Family

Crisis

Guidebook

Family Crisis Guidebook

Practical Steps to Work Through
Difficult Issues

Daniel Bates, LMHC

Longform
PUBLISHING
CREATIVE ENDEAVORS THAT MATTER

Other works by Daniel Bates

Even a Superhero Needs Counseling:
*What Superheroes and Supervillains
Teach Us About Ourselves*

Learning to Live:
*20 Lessons from a Therapist
on Learning to Live a Better Life*

When Parenting Backfires:
*Twelve Thinking Errors That Undermine
Parents' Effectiveness*
(Co-Authored with David Simonsen, PhD)

The Modern Mystic

ISBN: 0-9973115-8-7
ISBN 13: 978-0-9973115-8-7

Library of Congress Control Number: 2018909150

LCCN Imprint Name:
Longform Publishing, United States

At Longform Publishing, we are passionate about delivering high impact books from dynamic authors.

We publish books in the areas of mental health, self-help, Christian spirituality and growth, and personal development. Each book we release has our stamp of approval for being material that will not only entertain, but make you think. It is our mission to put for books that have the purpose and intention of doing good for the world and for each and every reader.

We encourage you to look at our website long-formpublishing.com and peruse each selection and find the one that fits what you are looking for.

Dedicated to families who are hurting, desperate for help, and willing to do the hard work in order to build better relationships.

Table of Contents

Introduction

This book will not save you. Only *you* can save you.

This book will not give you immediate fixes. It took years to create the problem your family is facing, and it may take years to fix it. It's going to take time and hard work. Looking for the quick and easy fix is a waste of time.

This book is not about building ammunition to use against an individual. It took a group effort to create this crisis and it's going to take a group effort to fix it. Team work, solidarity, individual family members working alongside each other are required.

This book will pull no punches. I am not going to play nice. I'm going to give you a healthy dose of "tough love." And that's done with a purpose. I've worked with enough families to know that people, even when they desperately want change, are wedded to notions that keep them stuck. To disabuse you of those keeping-you-stuck notions, you need to have your boat rocked. The *status quo* must be disrupted because what you've been doing — how your family has functioned up till now — isn't working.

And maybe, deep down, you know this to be true. But to state it out loud, in the presence of your family members, may seem frightening. So you pretend like there is no problem. You ignore the obvious. I call that denial. Plain and simple. And over time, denial only makes the problem worse until it builds up to a crisis.

You may realize that your family can no longer function in the way it has. When patterns playing out in your family are so unsatisfying, *not* changing is not an option. The cost of denying the problem is too great. And the stuck-ness becomes the *status quo*, and nothing ever changes, and the pain continues.

No more! You are reading this because you know something needs to change. If you want what you've always gotten, then do what you've always done. If you want something different, then you must do something different.

Change must occur in the attitudes, behaviors, mindsets, responses, strategies, coping mechanisms, schedules, routines, and habits of everyone in the family to achieve positive, healthy results. The family system, must operate differently. Nothing will change unless change occurs. The whole family can start with collective action, but even the positive changes of an individual family member can lead to a meaningful change in the way the family, as a system, functions.

Change is very uncomfortable, yet discomfort is useful. Discomfort challenges the *status quo* and motivates change. It's a good thing! Run towards discomfort instead of away. For change to occur in your family, you will have to be open to new ideas that may seem uncomfortable.

- You will have to be open to input from others.

- You will have to be humble.

- You will have to take risks and be vulnerable.

- You will have to own up to where you are at fault.

- You will have to break bad habits and learn new, positive habits.

And this book will help you do that and more! *This book will help you and your family overcome a relational, substance abuse, or mental health crisis.* For the last seven years, I've worked with families in the juvenile justice system and in my private practice, and let me tell you, what I just described above ain't easy. People get so focused on their hurt, on their pain, on their need to be right that they can't work together. They just want the *other* person to be fixed. I've worked with scores of families who couldn't get it, who refused to work together, who couldn't listen to each other, who couldn't stop blaming.

Working through a crisis as a family is hard work with a high failure rate. So why do it? Why even confront your problems and try to change? Well, I've also worked with enough families to know that change *is* possible. I have witnessed families get through hellish circumstances and come out better for it. I've seen families first-hand, face unimaginable crises and survive. Not only did they survive, but the crisis helped them to address deeper problems and see growth and change because of their hard work.

This book includes some of those stories of change and even a few stories of distress. They are meant to demonstrate that working your way out of a family crisis can be done and how to shift your thinking patterns. It can be done in such a way that you become better, happier, and healthier as a family than you were before the crisis started. Please know that the families introduced to you throughout this book have had their information regarding age, name, gender, and any other personally identifiable information for their protection. It is also possible that by reading this book, you realize your family needs more help than what you or this book can offer. That is why the last chapter of this book, chapter 11, walks you through the process of identifying when your family needs counseling, how you can find a counselor, what you can expect over the course of family counseling and how you and your family can make it successful as possible.

Change may seem impossible now, in the moment, but there is hope in the midst of what you are facing. Change will require the involvement of the whole family — family members cooperating, against a common enemy, for a common purpose. You'll have to trust each other, you'll have to stop blaming each other, and to take responsibility for their own actions. You'll have to forgive, learn new patterns of behavior--new ways of being. Yes, relationships are messy. Yes, family problems are complicated. But dysfunctional families can change. It is possible!

Chapter 1

The Crisis

The first thing you **must** understand about the crisis you are in: the crisis is *not the cause* of your pain and anguish. The crisis is *the symptom*.

What!

Your crisis is like the "Check Engine" light in the dashboard of your car. The crisis is an *indicator* of the issue or issues that have been at play for some time. The reason it's evident now is that the long-term issues have hit a threshold. The volcano of distress has been lying dormant, but ready to erupt. All it needed was a tipping point.

Therefore, it does you little good to focus solely on *how* the crisis started. That's a short-sighted focus. It's a *microscopic* perspective and won't lead to real change. You need to start looking at your family from a *macroscopic* point of view. Look at the big picture. That isn't to say seeing the big picture only leads to big change. It is the big picture approach that informs what and how to make small changes that help your family in the day-to-day as well as in the long-term.

It also does you no good to focus on *whom* the crisis started with. Placing blame on an individual distracts families from focusing on how the crisis interconnects everyone in the family and distracts from self-responsibility.

When you pull back and look at everything — your family history, which may include trauma, loss, or transitions; important events; repeated problematic behaviors — you can start to see patterns. Noticing those patterns are the key to getting out of this crisis. But, your vision, your ability to look at the big picture and notice the patterns of behavior in your family, is obscured when, like I said before, the focus of your attention is fixed on *how* the crisis started or *whom* it started with. You just get stuck and fail to move forward.

So I want you to do three things.

1 Take your focus off individuals. Stop blaming yourself or some other person, and ask yourself, *how is everyone involved in the problem?* Which should lead you into the next and very important question, what role am I playing in the problem? How am I contributing to the issue? Hopefully you will see that, as a colleague of mine has said when working with families, "no one is to blame, but everyone is responsible."[1]

Everyone contributes to the problem in one way or another. Some more. Some less. But regardless of who you are, you're involved.[2]

Stop blaming one person, and let's focus on dynamics in the family. Chapter 2 will address the problems of an individual focus and provide solutions.

2 Take your focus off how the crisis started. Stop looking for an event, that is, a single cause. Families reach a crisis point, depending on what the crisis is, over a period of time. Problems don't spring into being overnight. It takes a lot of practice to get things wrong. Therefore, you need to readjust your perspective. You need to start paying attention to patterns of behavior and stop focusing on individual behavior. Chapter 3 will go into more depth about these patterns.

---

[1] Will Schultz (quote slightly changed)

[2] This is true in the majority of family issue. It is not true, however, in cases of unidirectional domestic violence and abuse. Please see *Appendix A* for more information on the nature of domestic violence and abuse, and what immediate action's you can take if you are in an abusive relationship to help your situation.

3 Finally, your family will never escape this crisis until you start being honest with each other. Families can fall anywhere on the honesty spectrum. Some families are so afraid of conflict, they never address the 400-pound gorilla in the room. And maybe, if someone challenges the *norm*, even if it's awful and needs to be changed, the family will silence that person. The family might hold a strong belief that one person is the cause of the issue, yet never able to admit to their own roles in the problem. Other families fall somewhere in between these two extremes.

The goal for your family ought to be honesty. The *well-worn patterns*, your ego, the egos of others, and your fears of conflict can no longer stand as excuses. Something has to change. And the only way to get different results is to do something different. If you can't commit to this step, then stop reading. You'll have to get a bit uncomfortable for this process to work. The life of your family depends on all of you committing to this new focus.

It is essential that everyone shift the focus from one of blame to a sense of shared responsibility and ownership of the problem. Change must be a collaborative effort in order to get everyone onboard and to marshal the collective effort of each family member. Stop blaming each other. If everyone makes an honest examination of their behavior, responses, habits, and intentions, transformation occurs.

It is essential that everyone start listening to each other. The only way you are going to get out of this crisis is with each other. You can't run away from your family — even though you may be mad or hurt or scared. Cutting your family out of your life doesn't cut their influence from your living. Unresolved family issues are sticky. They don't just go away because we don't like them.

The crisis presents you and your family with two hurdles: paralysis or effort with little reward. The only way to overcome these obstacles is if you work together, in unison. You must use the crisis and the difficulty it presents to unify, or you will turn on each other. When you listen and try to understand the other person's point of view or feedback, even when you disagree, you have a fighting chance. It took all of you to get into this mess; it's going to take all of you to get out of it.

Chapter 2

Identify the REAL Problem

Families make two critical errors when they are trying to understand and work their way out of a crisis. These errors are difficult to identify because they are disguised under the veneer of common sense. So, in order to recognize the errors for what they are, you and your family must be open to a new perspective. This may require everyone to take a deep breath and do some investigating because it is simply lazy to run with an overly simplistic, negative and blaming understanding of a problem that relates to something as intricate and nuanced as a family system. Reality bears out that family crises are rarely concluded with the words "She did it!" As you will see in this chapter, family problems and crises are not quick and easy to understand. Everyone's story and perspective must be understood and valued in order to gain sufficient knowledge of what is going on.

So what are these two errors?

1 Families that place all the blame for what they see as the problem on the shoulders of one person ensure the problem will continue. What makes this so damaging? Let's think about responsibility from a purely rational point of view, take feelings out of it. It is logically impossible for one person to always be at fault for something.

There's a concept shared by those who study how systems work in biology, business, and economics called *reciprocal feedback loop.* In simple language, no action or behavior is isolated. Everything is connected. Much like the cliché example of the butterfly flapping its wings in the Amazon causing a hurricane in the Caribbean. It's a chain reaction. Families operate similarly. In the family context, one person's behavior has an impact on the other members who respond, and in turn those members impact others who respond, and so on and so forth.

One person's behavior (healthy or unhealthy) has an impact on other family members and elicits a certain response (which could also be healthy or unhealthy). That being said, remember everyone is responsible for their own behavior and their own responses. This means that unhealthy behaviors don't just beget unhealthy responses, they can be met with healthy responses that prohibit a continuation of the starting behavior.

Accepting this idea means your family understands that the responsibility for the problem is shared. Members in the family contribute, all in their own way and to varying degrees, to the problem. The problem is contained within a relational context. The metaphor often used by family therapists is the kinetic mobile. Typically seen in baby nurseries or holding various photos, the design is simple. A string or wire is connected to a lever that is counterweighted, which is connected to another lever, and to another. The result is a series of levers dangling from one string or wire in perfect balance. If one lever moves ever so slightly, all the other levers are affected. The way one lever affects the balance held by all the levers is much like the balance held in families – you affect one, you affect them all

The actions of each member of the family affect the other members of the family: the success of an older sibling viewed with resentment by a jealous younger sibling who covets the attention of his parents; a daughter traumatized by the sexual molestation of her uncle and her parents blame each intensely that they divorced; three sons develop serious drug addictions to cope with the constant fighting and unhealthy communication of their parents; a wife seeks out the attention of another man and begins an affair because her husband's lack of emotional expressiveness and affection leaves her feeling emotionally deprived. These are painful scenarios with deeply wounding patterns and yet no one scenario has one person contributing solely to the hurt.

| Family Story | I once worked with a couple, Imani and Shanice, who adopted two young girls, Alexus and Carly out of the foster care system. The two girls, unbeknownst to the new parents, were experiencing a disorder called *Reactive Attachment Disorder*. One symptom of the disorder is an inability to express and receive love with a primary caregiver. When Imani and Shanice tried to build an emotional connection with their daughters by giving them hugs, verbally affirming them, experiencing fun activities together (the behaviors), Alexus and Carly wouldn't and couldn't receive their love (the response). Imani and Shanice in turn felt like they were bad parents and doubted themselves (response) rendering the couple to feelings of hopelessness and defeat. Attempts at building the emotional bond with their kids diminished (behavior) resulting in Alexus and Carly's further withdrawal (response). Because Imani and Shanice didn't have a full understanding of what was going on (i.e. the big picture), they unjustly blamed themselves without realizing that their adopted daughters undiagnosed disorder was the cause, wreaking havoc on their attempts to form a meaningful relationship. Other parents, in similar situations, blame the kids for the

rocky relationship. Regardless of where the blame is directed (self or other), the shift in perspective to blame ceases the pursuit to go deeper, to find a fair and true explanation for the relational crisis.

2 The second error that families make is hyper-focusing on events instead of patterns. Most of the time I hear families describe the problem a past event. Invariably, there was something that happened years ago, like an accident, death of a loved one, drug overdose, an incident of domestic violence, betrayal, or job loss that affected the family in a powerful way. In other words, they identify a very serious past event with an ongoing emotional impact or "Because of that event, we now have these problems."

The events families describe to me *are* very serious. They are noteworthy. They are meaningful and influential to the present. They are deeply emotional and important to acknowledge *and* they are not the root of the issue. In honest moments, family members recognize their issues had been present for some time. The crisis event just birthed the reality.

For example, think about building a fire. You start with a small flame, but it's not big enough to provide heat or to cook with., so you add fuel. Lighter fluid goes onto the fire and — whoosh! — the fire is going strong. The lighter fluid did not create the fire, but it did intensify the flame. Major events that happen in the life of a family are like the lighter fluid — they don't cause the problems, they just intensify them. When you put all your focus on the event that only manifested the problem, you aren't dealing with the *real* problem. The event only made the problem impossible to ignore.

If you want to see real change in your family life, as a family you need to identify the real problem. You can no longer let the circumstantial events be a distraction. The *real* problem can take many different shapes and forms, depending on the family. But the common denominator for every real family problem is a *toxic pattern of behavior.*

| Family Story | Troy and Terri were parents struggling with their teenage son, Nick, who experienced legal trouble after committing vandalism in his neighborhood. The family's reaction was severe, which led to conflict, and ultimately provided key insight into this family's bigger issues. The family blamed the vandalism as the start of everything. And if only the son hadn't done what he had done, they wouldn't be fighting like they were. Because the family held to the idea that it ignited the family distress, I had to work to confront and demonstrate to the trio that the family issues were at play before the son's vandalism. The incident magnified the issues already present thus presenting an opportunity. The incident escalated the family's issues to the point that they recognized the need for outside help and for changes. In fact, the family admitted that they would have never sought out a counselor if the incident had not occurred. They would have

continued "putting up with it." But now that everything was out in the open — the real problems now being obvious and undeniable — they had the chance to work on them and hope for positive change, something they very much wanted. This crisis helped bring their issues into the light and allowed us to work on them and see change through counseling.

Finish this chapter with hope — hope that when you stop individualizing and attributing your family problems to a specific incident, you will be able to see the toxic patterns from a relational perspective. It's in this perspective that you'll be able to make serious and lasting change in your family life. That's the silver lining in your family crisis. Take heart and have hope.

Chapter 3

The Necessity of Reframing

Maybe you're open to shifting from the individualized / event focus to the relational/ pattern focus, but you're not fully convinced. You're open but still skeptical. When serious hurt, broken trust, and relational damage has accrued over time in families, it's very difficult to break away from the blame you may have for your dad, mom, son, daughter, brother, sister, or extended family member. It's extremely difficult to give up your hurt. Yet, there is a dark side to un-relinquished hurt, it restricts your vision.

Imagine that you are on a train. As you're going along the track, you can see everything: forests, rivers, mountains, towns, and cities. Then you enter a tunnel, and your vision goes dark. All you can see is the light at the end of the tunnel and what that light illuminates. This narrows your vision dramatically. All you perceive is what you can see. This narrowed field of vision is called *tunnel vision.*

Tunnel vision is dangerous. It limits vision to selectively rule out uncomfortable facts, which may be vital for family members to see and acknowledge. And no family is immune to being guilty of tunnel vision. It can affect any kind of family regardless of nationality, culture, religion, or era. In the analogy, you have no choice in what you are blind to due to the nature of being in a dark tunnel. However, in the context of the family; tunnel vision is a choice. Family members intentionally focus on what they want to see and dismiss what they don't want to see.

If unchecked, tunnel vision can cause great relational harm and keep families stuck in negative patterns. If a dad selectively focuses on what his child does wrong and dismisses what his child does right, this will lead to much resentment and conflict. If a stepdaughter only sees her stepdad doting on his biological kids but ignores the various ways he tries to build a relationship with her, she invalidates his efforts and welcomes further drift. If a mom focuses aggressively on how her daughter parents differently than she, she risks overlooking the positive and innovative ways her daughter manages her children.

So the million-dollar question is, how does a family fix the tunnel-vision problem?

We all erect, what psychologists have termed, *mental frameworks* around our experiences. Mental frameworks provide a structure for understanding and interpreting our lives. And it is our mental frameworks which are negatively impacted by the effects of tunnel vision. For example, let's say you're texting a friend. You mention something about a new project you are working on. They don't respond. You wait for their response, but still, nothing. As more time elapses you begin to worry that they aren't responding because they hate your project. You become so consumed by this fear that you abandon the project and vow to never share your ideas with another person again. Then, a few minutes later, your friend texts you back to say they love the project. They praise your creativity and imagination and ask to see more of it. Whoops! You realize how foolish your reaction was and continue the conversation with your friend.

Isn't it curious how our minds hurry toward negative assumptions when people don't respond to us right away? Why did we do that? The answer has to do with the frameworks in which we house our experiences.

Frameworks hurt us when we base them on faulty and insufficient information, on assumptions and hasty conclusions.[3] Faulty frameworks force us

---

[3] To learn more about problems in our mental frameworks, also called thinking errors, and how they can harm a family system when unchecked, see *Appendix C*.

to respond to others in negative and unhealthy ways that only hurt us and our relationships. It is, therefore, healthy to challenge your frameworks and see if there is any reason to *re-frame* your view of other people's behavior.

How to Reframe

1 First, identify *alternative explanations* for your family member's hurtful behavior. Try to see the positive intention behind a family member's unwise action. It is very easy to jump to an erroneous or negative conclusion because we get to be the "victim." It feels good (in a wrong sort of way) to be the grieved party and to have something over the wrongdoer's head. We can inflict punishment, manipulate with our newfound leverage, or just lord it over them. What may feel good in the moment, only leads to a harmful effect to the family in the long-run.

Family Story | I once worked with a family where Darrius and his son, Terrance, got into awful fights. Neither of them listened to the other and they spoke to each other aggressively, with hostility in their voices and body language. But after years of metaphorically beating their heads against each other, Terrance grew tired of the fights. Terrance chose to walk away from heated conversations with his dad. He wanted to prevent the conversation going too far.

Surprisingly, this strategy increased the escalation. Why? When Terrance walked away, Darrius interpreted that action as a sign of disrespect, which made him even more furious and more hostile towards his son. Isn't it curious that Darrius came to this conclusion about the intentions of his son when he walked away? Let's look at Darrius' framework.

When Terrance walked away, Darrius took that behavior as a dismissal of his opinion. He thought his son was demonstrating disrespect. This infuriated Darrius and he became more hostile and aggressive as a result. When I worked with the family, I suggested to Dad that his son wasn't disrespecting him by walking away — he was, in fact, trying to de-escalate the conversation. Even more, Terrance respected his dad enough to cut off an unhealthy conversation that would normally lead to a physical altercation. Walking away from the conversation was an attempt to preserve the relationship.

At first Darrius didn't buy what I was selling. The framework he built around his son's behavior wouldn't allow for such an interpretation. Walking away from heated conversations was a clear sign of disrespect. But with time and after some good conversation about respect, the son's positive intent, the destructive nature of their heated arguments, and ways to de-escalate, Dad accepted a new framework that made space for his son's positive intent. Darrius reframed his son's withdrawal as positive. This helped the two of them realize they were on the same side. They both wanted to avoid escalated fights. And when Terrance walked away, Dad no longer became furious.

One good thing led to another. When they understood each other's frameworks, they were able to acknowledge how the other person perceived them in a negative light. Terrance was able to see, given Dad's framework, how his actions could be seen as disrespectful. And Dad could see, given his son's framework, that his son's intentions were respectful when he walked away.

Seeing each other in a new light helped them communicate in calmer, more respectful ways. They didn't feel so attacked because they knew where the other was coming from. This new experience gave them something they never had before: hope. They weren't out of the woods yet. The duo still had a lot of hard work to do — but at least they were headed in the right direction.

2 Second, consider your family member's behavior as their misguided *way of dealing with their own pain.* This is another contour of looking for alternative explanations of a family members poor behavior that is not overly simplistic and negative. The other benefit is that if, by looking for it, you can understand your dad's or sister's hurtful behavior towards you as a mislead way of dealing with a problem, well, can't you relate with that? Haven't you ever made a poor choice because you didn't know how to deal with a problem? Haven't you ever done something you regret because your judgment was clouded by emotional pain? Of course, you can. We call can. We've all been in that place. It doesn't excuse the wrongness of the behavior, but it also doesn't mean it was a coldhearted, malicious act, done with malevolent intent. We may want to think that, at first, but that is our own pain talking. And if it is true, they behaved badly because of their pain or hurt, a negative response from you out of your own hurt and hurt, only furthers the cycle. An opportunity to powerfully change the course of your family by extending yourself beyond a sense of outrage, and to show them compassion for their pain, is seized when you assume this perspective.

I once worked with Jake and his
| Family Story | daughter Katelyn in family therapy. After repeated requests by Jake and for Kate to complete her chores, Jake became upset at Kate's repeated lack of follow through. When she did do her chores, Jake shared that Katelyn was incredibly slow in completing them. Being a single dad, he felt like his daughter was being selfish: a negative interpretation of the daughter's intention based on her behavior. He felt like she didn't care, she was only concerned about her own agenda. This was especially frustrating for him because he was working two jobs, raising two kids, and receiving counseling in order to get his family help. He felt like he had to do everything himself, and his kids weren't helping. When Jake shared these things, Katelyn would become furious and shut down — her typical response when feeling attacked.

As counseling progressed, I built a good relationship with Katelyn, which lead to her sharing more without shutting down. She explained, and her father confirmed, that after her mom died, Jake remarried a woman, Carol. The relationship between Katelyn and her new step-mom was cordial at first, but quickly took a turn for the worse. Things got so bad between the two of them, Katelyn would try to sabotage whatever she did just to aggravate Carol. Carol's response to her step-daughter became increasingly rage-fueled and abusive. Years later, Jake decided to leave Carol for a number of reasons.

Hearing this additional background data helped me reframe Katelyn's behaviors. Even though Carol was gone, and even though Dad was in no way as rigid, militant, or stern as she had been — he was in fact patient and reasonable in his expectations — the trauma Katelyn experienced at the hands of Carol still lingered. Dad agreed this was the case and I introduced the concept that Katelyn's trauma was manifesting itself in various ways. The home-life structure itself (doing chores, going to school, going to bed, etc.) acted as a trigger for the daughter. This meant that Katelyn, on an unconscious level, would feel anxious, overwhelmed, or afraid of embarrassment and shame if she didn't accomplish the chore perfectly. Thus leading to her patterns of shutting down. Meanwhile, all Dad saw was on the surface was his daughter either shirking her chores.

I shared with Jake that Katelyn's behavior was not about sabotaging him, even though it looked and felt as such. It wasn't done selfishly. Katelyn, unconsciously, had associated the normal structure of daily living in the home with her past traumatic experience. So when she went to do a chore, she felt as if she were back in that abusive situation. The point of identifying this was not to excuse her behavior,clearly, she has a responsibility to do her chores,,but to highlight the fact that Katelyn's experience is *relatable*, that there was in fact no malicious intent behind her actions. Jake could relate with Katelyn's urge to shut down; he too suffered from feeling overwhelmed, scared, afraid, anxious, or ashamed following his first wife's death and at the hands of his alcoholic and abusive second wife.

After exploring this concept, Jake felt great empathy for Katelyn after being able to create a framework for the situation and the anger and resentment he felt for her lack of follow-through dissipated. They were able to have a meaningful, vulnerable, and real conversation filled with empathy and understanding Obviously, this reframing didn't fix all their problems. But it did allow them to have a meaningful conversation from which they walked away understanding one other. Once Katelyn felt like she was heard and understood by her dad, she apologized for not doing her chores and she too understood her father's a heartfelt pain. She was able to share how grateful she was for his hard work to provide for them-a comment that brought Jake to tears.

Addressing these deep-felt issues cleared the way for the family to discuss practical matters like chores without any hidden issues sabotaging their discussion. I know it's not easy to do. It can be challenging to see family members who have hurt you in new ways. Yet, the benefits of reframing are real. Reframing can help repair and restore relationships.

Chapter 4

Changing Family Patterns

How do you change a toxic pattern of behavior? It requires an honest understanding of what the toxic pattern of behavior is, who does what, and what are its results. The first step in changing problem patterns is *recognition*.

You can't fight an enemy you don't know exists, can you? You can't change a toxic pattern of behavior plaguing your family that you haven't identified. Recognizing patterns allows families to make meaningful choices in how they behave. Without recognition, families are enslaved to vicious cycles.

An unrecognized toxic pattern of behavior controls a family who might otherwise control themselves.

| Family Story |

In the case of Patricia and her daughter Cheryl, the family dynamics contributed to Cheryl's addiction struggles. Patricia was solely emotionally dependent on Cheryl which left her feeling like her needs weren't being met and that she wasn't valued or even loved. This pattern of Patricia's unwillingness to allow Cheryl a voice in their relationship, contributed to Cheryl's hidden addictions and her legal troubles.

Cheryl felt trapped and emotionally suffocated by her mother's emotional dependence on her. She started drinking, using drugs, acting out sexually; whatever it took to feel good she would do. And it worked, temporarily. When she had sex, she felt loved. When she gave her money to friends, she felt appreciated. When she injected heroin into her veins, she felt at peace. Pretty soon, these risky behaviors became a lifestyle of addiction. She couldn't stop. She was addicted to drugs and owed a great deal of money to her dealers which then led to prostitution and even legal troubles. Patricia found out what was really going on after the police and drug dealers began visiting her home. Patricia accused her daughter of shifting the blame when Cheryl explained she felt like her needs weren't being met, that she simply wanted to feel valued and loved. And so, Cheryl continued using, continuing the toxic pattern.

This is a harrowing story of a mother and daughter unable to break free from a cycle of guilt, blame and addiction. The commitment to change as in the case of Patricia and Cheryl, and in most families, would ideally be an effort involving everyone. The more family members onboard, the more change that can be achieved. That is not to say an individual, making changes in how they respond to their family members, can't have a meaningful impact on their family system. They can. But change is much easier when, as much as possible, the entire family is committed.

Sometimes, those in the family who feel the most hurt or anger or disconnection think they bear less responsibility for change — after all, they are the ones who are hurt. They think everyone *else* needs to change only when everyone else starts making changes, will they too change. The problem? Usually, everyone in the family feels wounded, ensuring a standstill. Think of the vultures in Disney's version of *The Jungle Book* when they keep asking each other "what do you want to do?" and the response is "I dunno. What do you want to do?" Notice they don't actually *do* anything because no one is willing to break the cycle.

We all have reasons why *we* aren't the ones who need change. Change requires family members to trust each other. Change requires the family environment to be emotionally safe. For example, imagine two people stand just slightly apart, back to back, to do a trust fall exercise. On the count of three, both people fall backwards, trusting that the other person is also falling backwards to stop gravity's downward pull. But if one person decides not to fall backwards in unison with the other, the trusting person will fall back and smack their head on the ground. No one wants to be the person on the ground with a head injury. No one wants to put forth effort and trust if the other members of their family won't also do the same. Creating environment of emotional safety, where attempts to change are more likely to happen, is the responsibility of everyone, even the person who thinks they bear the least responsibility to change.

So, stop looking for someone to blame.

Stop putting yourself in a place of moral superiority.

Do what you can to be encouraging.

Do what you can so those in your family feel the courage to take a risk and try something new. Yet your family wants to expend their energy — and trying new things is an emotionally costly activity — you want your family attempting change with the highest likely of sustained change, as possible. So, in order to ensure everyone's efforts is in unison and maximized for the greatest benefits, the follow 5 steps will help with that aim.

Step 1: Identify the typical triggers of the toxic pattern of behavior.

Step 2: Identify what everyone does when the cycle of conflict is triggered.

Step 3: Identify the results of the toxic pattern.

Step 4: Identify the positive results you want.

Step 5: Create both strategies of prevention and redirection.

1 Identify what typically triggers the toxic pattern of behavior. Triggers, in the family context, are *expectations, circumstances, and behaviors* that initiate the toxic pattern of behavior. For example, a parent antici-pates coming home to find that their kid has com-pleted all the assigned chores (expectation). When they come home to find the chores incomplete (cir-cumstance), they become irritated. That irritation turns into resentment as they ponder how hard they work and how little effort their child puts into what's asked of them. But instead of confronting their child, instead of yelling at them, the par-ent stews (behavior) on that resentment for hours. Then, the child asks to do something they've been permitted to do a thousand times before, like go-ing to a friend's house. "No." says the parent. The child protests, complaining that their parent is being inconsistent and "unfair." The parent hangs on to that word *unfair*. And then the floodgates are opened. The parent launches salvo after salvo at their child for not pulling their weight around the house, for being ungrateful, and for demand-ing privileges that the parent didn't get when they were a child because they had to work and help out around the house. At this point, the child be-comes infuriated at the attack and launches back at the parenting, pointing out all their flaws. And on and on it goes, playing out like it has always played out, over and over again, and reaching the same results: hurt, anger, resentment, and unresolved tension.

Take a moment and think of how your family's toxic pattern of behavior typically starts. Identify: what are the expectations, circumstances, and behaviors involved?

2 Identify what everyone *does* after the toxic pattern of behavior has been triggered, in an objective behavioral sense. What do I mean by this? It is easy to go down rabbit trails when trying to accurately describe a toxic pattern of behavior. It is easy to get distracted by whatever intent was behind your actions. But for this step, I just want you to focus on what the behavior is. It is important to focus on behavior, regardless of intent, because family members react to one another based on each other's actions. Each must own the consequences of their behavior. Others can't see your intentions, but they can see how you behave and will react based on that. There's a place for discussing your intent and clarifying why you did what you did. But this isn't the time for that. At this stage, everyone must take responsibility for how their behavior affects everyone else.

3 Identify the results of the pattern. Typically, toxic patterns of behavior lead to bad outcomes: an isolated family member, drug use, poor decision making, a call to the police. And these are results no one in the family wants. That's important for everyone to recognize. The outcome of the conflict leaves no true winner. It is a lose–lose situation.

Maybe you feel justified in your behavior in the moment, but it's important to realize that you don't actually like the consequences of the toxic family pattern. You're likely unaware of it now, but you must come to see how your behavior contributes to these outcomes. And if there is change you can make, be open to what that change is.

4 You have identified the results you don't want; now it's time to identify the results you do want. Ask yourself, *if my family's toxic pattern could be changed so as to lead to a positive outcome, what would that positive outcome be?* Everyone listens to each other despite disagreement? Everyone stops blaming and engages in effective problem-solving? I want you to dream a little with each other. Take the focus away from how things go wrong, and imagine how they could go right. It's a helpful question that can spark some brainstorming. This is a short step, but an important one.

5 Finally, create two types of strategies. First, create a strategy of *trigger-prevention* so the toxic pattern of behavior can't get rolling in the first place. Second, create a strategy of *redirection* to execute when the toxic pattern of behavior is triggered, a kind of family fail-safe. Your strategies should be sufficient to stop the old pattern from playing out

its full cycle. They should aim at redirecting the family's focus to achieve the ideal outcomes you identified in the Step 4.

In review, your family's job is to: Step 1: Identify the typical triggers of the toxic pattern of behavior. Step 2: Identify what everyone does when the cycle of conflict is triggered. Step 3: Identify the results of the toxic pattern. Step 4: Identify the positive results you want. Step 5: Create both strategies of prevention and redirection.

It's so simple, right? I say that facetiously. It really is hard work and will take time to master. You may need outside help to work through all the steps, but I attest to their effectiveness. Families have seen real benefits from working through this method for change. Just allow time and effort as you work through it. Change won't come immediately, but it will come.

Chapter 5

Creating Positive Communication Patterns

The key way to break toxic patterns of behavior is to either *prevent* the toxic pattern of behavior being triggered or to *redirect* the toxic pattern of behavior to desired, positive outcomes. Prevention and redirection are not possible if a family cannot positively and constructively communicate with each other. Healthy communication provides the foundation and the means for stopping toxic patterns and creating healthy ones. In this chapter, I will address how families can: communicate, listen, negotiate, give and receive feedback, fight fairly, and de-escalate heated arguments.

How to Communicate

Good communication is much more difficult and entails far more effort than is required to communicate poorly. Many pages could be filled as to why this is true, but for you and your family, the first focus should be on what good communication is and how can you practice it. The ability to communicate effectively is the basis for any meaningful work on family issues. If you can't communicate with each other, how are you ever to discuss the problem and work on a solution?

1 Be brief. When you grandstand, the door opens for defensiveness or the idea that the others involved in the dialogue must protect themselves. When you pile on several unnecessary examples to support your perspective, that are difficult for your dialogue partner to hear, you can create an atmosphere of defensiveness. When too many extraneous details are provided, you run the risk of losing people's attention. Furthermore, lecturing creates the risk of the other communicator feeling belittled and disrespected. You can thankfully avoid all these problems with brevity. It may sound artificial, but hold yourself to just a few statements. Try getting your point across in three sentences.

2 Good communication focuses on behaviors and not on negative judgments. For example, let's say your teen lied about where they were over the weekend. They said they were with a friend who they know you approve of, but instead they were with a friend who does not have your approval. When talking with them, be sure to focus on the behavior and not on a negative judgement. If you call your child a *liar*, that's a label, and labels come with several problems such as disengagement and defensiveness. A description of *what* your child did that was wrong increases the likelihood of engaging them in a real discussion about lying and the negative impact it has on the trust between you and them. Make sure to emphasize that building trust is in their interest. They get more freedom when there is a solid foundation of trust between you. Secondly, describing *what* your child did wrong versus describing *them* as wrong, circumvents the problems of them taking your remarks personally. In summary, discuss the problematic behavior, *lying*, avoiding a negative description of their identity, *liar*. As a result, your child will be less reactive, and you will increase the likelihood that they will listen and engage with what you say.[4]

---

[4] For a longer discussion on this point, see my book When Parenting Backfires, which is described at the end of this book in the More About the Author section.

3 Watch what your body is saying. Body language communicates just as much as your words through posture, eye contact, facial expressions. So, make sure your body matches the content of one's words. If you are apologizing — but you're rolling your eyes with hands on your hips, tapping your foot impatiently — others are going to think the apology is disingenuous. Body language often betrays the true feelings of the communicator. But sometimes we unintentionally communicate something with body language that we truly didn't mean to communicate. For example, a son comes to his dad with an idea he's very excited about. The dad listens to the idea and is very quiet, looks down at his feet, and scratches his head. The son perceives his dad's lack of excitement as disapproval and walks away feeling rejected. Later the father learns of his son's feelings and is surprised. He didn't intend to shoot down his son's idea at all; in fact, he was giving it heavy thought because he took his son's idea seriously. So we ought to be mindful of not only what we are communicating with our words, but also with our bodies.

Todd was a man who demanded | Family Story | respect. When his son Branden would pushback on his request, Todd became enraged. He'd take any opportunity to tell his son, at great length, how he should be respectful and thoughtful when speaking to his father. Todd grew up with a father who demanded respect and severe punishment followed any back talking. And he was not about to give Branden any passes. As he would explain with Branden, he would get carried away. The communication between them became a one-sided lecture and inevitably, over the course of the conversation Branden would mentally check-out. This only angered Todd more.

When I started working with the father-son duo, I mentioned that Todd had wise and important information to share with his son, but the power of his words was ultimately rendered impotent due to his grandstanding, casting negative judgments at his son, and is being rather aggressive with his body language. He was trying to control versus influence his son.

I coached him to be brief, use behaviorally descriptive language (instead of negative judgments), and to approach Branden less aggressively with his non-verbal communication. I then challenged him to try these new behaviors to see if Branden would be more receptive. He implemented my suggestions and noticed that Branden stopped checking-out mid-conversation. Branden started paying more attention to what his dad had to say more importantly, he began responding to his dad. This showed Todd that his son was actually understanding what he said to him. Talk about a huge win for the father-son duo. This set the foundation for further, healthy communication between the two.

How to Listen

Families fall into common pitfalls when they get into arguments. These pitfalls create hurt. Not listening, arguing just to be found right, attacking, accusing, bringing up past mistakes, and blowing up or shutting down — these feel right in the moment, but in the long-term, they negatively impact family relationships. Whatever the pitfalls you find yourself prone to, change starts with you. You must lead the way to a better relationship by learning to listen.

I have found that some families are very good at getting their points across, which is a great strength. But good self-expression doesn't always lead to good conversations. The missing piece is listening. Speaking and listening are two sides of the same communication coin. Here are some practical steps for better listening.

1 Listen to what the other person is saying in order to understand their experience. This requires you to see from their point of view, even if you disagree with what they are saying at the outset of the conversation. Understanding the other person is not a conceit. You can still disagree with the other person. You can still hold to your position. But, you hold onto to your position while making an effort to understand their position, too. So, close your mouth, and open your ears. Simply remaining silent is not good listening. Specifically, you have to try to understand what the other person felt and why they felt that way from their perspective. Once you have a sufficient understanding of their perspective, you must demonstrate your understanding through the use of a reflective statement, in which the listener reflects back the feelings of the speaker and the reasons given for those feelings.

Here's a script you can follow: "You feel... [name of the emotion] because... [reasons for the emotion]."

This is a handy script to follow to help you listen and express what you've understood. Sharing in the perspectives, experiences, opinions, and/or any other ideas of another person is deeply important when tackling the family crisis. It's about listening the other person, not building a case against them. Oftentimes, family members "listen" only as an attempt to seek out the weak spot in the other's argument. When you do this, your conversations will end in disaster. Instead, create understanding in your conversations or conflicts and they will succeed. Empathizing is essential to listening understand their perspective, experience, opinion, or any other ideas they are needing to share, only *then can you* articulate that understanding back.

2 More than likely, when using the skill, you captured the gist of what the person was trying to get across, but no one is perfect and you may have missed an important detail. A *clarifying question* is helpful in that it allows the speaker to address any missed issues you failed to bring up in your reflective listening statement. Clarification allows the other person to clear up a misunderstanding, to add extra information or to correct you. Clarification is a gesture of respect, and it helps families get on the same page. If you have done the hard work of understanding, articulating your understanding of what the other person shared, and clarifying any misunderstandings, then and only then, may you offer your side of the story. How you handle yourself during this phase makes or breaks the conversation. And it has a positive reciprocal effect in that they will be more likely to return the favor to you.

Here are few examples of clarifying questions: "Did I get that right?" "Was there anything I missed?" "What am I missing?"

3 Another dimension of effective listening is to share your feelings regarding what the other person said. This lets them know you are listening, but, more importantly, what they said has an emotional impact. Their experience registers an emotion with you. Be careful to not make sharing your feelings about you. You are sharing your feelings as it relates to what they said and their experience. Why does this matter? Imagine if you did a good functional job of listening, without expressing how their statements impacted you — you'd sound like a robot. Share how it hurts you to hear about your mom's sadness. Share how you are disheartened that your brother felt disrespected. Share how you feel frustrated that your aunt felt dismissed. Let's look at an example of how you do this by using the **"I" Statement script: "I feel... [name of the emotion]**

because... [reasons for the emotion]."

Listening can be hard and takes

| Family Story | self-control, practice, and patience. This is true for many and it was true for the Johnson family. Everyone in the family excelled at using their voice, making sure they were heard, and getting their point across, but their conversation usually led to dead ends. They all spoke *at* each other or *over* each other. It seemed like no one ever walked away from their conversations with a great understanding of each other. So much so, the problems raised were never resolved.

When I started working with the family the first thing I identified was the family's ability to express themselves and everyone collectively struggled in the listening department. They were great communicators, but poor listeners. I asked them to focus on what the other person was saying, to identify what the other person was feeling, and to verbalize their understanding of what the other person said. While it was shaky at first, and required active coaching, the family became better at listening. As a result, when everyone felt heard, their intensity dramatically reduced. They each felt more respected, validated and understood. Communication became safe and constructive.

How to Negotiate

Negotiation, in the family context, is the art of getting what you want or need without hurting relationships. Since families are composed of individuals who have wants and needs that may interfere with those of others, negotiation is a skill necessary for families to function effectively. When individual desires conflict, family members easily turn on each other. But when negotiation is done right, individuals can meet their needs without the expense of another. Below are four steps for effective family negotiation.

1 Identify your negotiables — things you are willing to budge on — and non-negotiables — things you are not willing to budge on. Be prepared to voice the reasons you aren't willing to budge on certain issues in a safe and healthy manner (refer to the previous section if needed). Furthermore, prepare to stick to your guns without becoming reactive, something that requires you to be clear, consistent, and calm. If you aren't clear, then the conversation will crumble into confusion. If you aren't consistent, your negotiation partner might call you out and lose respect or struggle to understand your convictions. If you aren't calm, the issue will never be discussed properly- you'll be too busy fighting.

2 Briefly state what you *want*. Don't give a long speech on your wish, why you want it, and why you should have it. Simply make your will known and let the other person have time to consider and respond to your claim. Know that you should be prepared to give more information if requested and to potentially share your perspective of why you should get what you want. Remember to be patient, if you become impatient and demanding, you are no longer negotiating — you're asking for relational damage.

3 Allow the other person to make a counteroffer. Another term for this exchange of offers is *bartering*. Bartering operates under the principle of *quid pro quo*, a Latin expression that means "something for something." In order to get something, you have to be willing to give up something else. For example, if a teenager wants to spend the weekend at a friend's house, a parent may say no. But if the parent and teenager were willing to negotiate, the teenager might barter additional chores for the privilege of going to a friend's house. The teenager gets to go to his friend's house, and the parent gets some additional chores done: win–win! Both sides get something from the negotiation.

4 Another equally important aspect of negotiation is *compromise*. Compromise requires some flexibility. If you are too rigid in your position, never considering the position of the other, you're likely to create resentment and resistance. Failure to be flexible could possibly hinder future negotiation because opportunities for the other person to reflect your previous rigidity arise. Be flexible and open to compromise because you might not get a **100** percent of what you want. It's still likely that you can get **80** percent, or even **50** percent, of your desired goal. Something is better than nothing.

| Family Story | Every time Candace and her son, Robert, encountered a problem, their efforts to communicate usually led to an impasse. Robert wanted what he wanted and Candace was the same way. Both were stubborn and unwilling to budge. As you can imagine, the duo grew tired of every disagreement becoming a battle.

When they reached out for my help, I suggested that Robert and Candace's greatest strength was stubbornness. I meant that with all sincerity. Stubbornness is a great interpersonal asset, when used in the right context, but in the wrong context, it can lead to interpersonal ruin. This is how they approached every conflict or disagreement with a "winner-take-all" mindset, leading to a no-win outcome for either of them. When asked about alternatives to their "winner-take-all" approach, neither one could. I suggested and explained a negotiation approach to help them collaborate with each other to reach a mutually amicable solution.

Walking them through the steps of negotiation, I pointed out that disagreements are opportunities to not only use negotiation skills, but opportunities to practice teamwork. Regardless of the outcome, if both feel like they are on the same team and indeed working together, the feeling of a united front will only help their relationship. Both Candace and Robert started using healthy negotiation skills and noticed that the conflicts didn't become arguments. The conversations felt better during and after because both Robert and Candace were able to strive towards a compromise.

How to Give and Receive Feedback

Effective feedback is when a family member points out a problem with another family members' behavior in a manner that is honoring and respectful. It's meant to be constructive, not destructive. When done right, feedback can help families in a powerful way to make positive changes. In fact, it is an act of love to give someone you care about constructive feedback given with the intention to help them and better the relationship. If you didn't care about them, you wouldn't bother giving the feedback, at all. The following steps will help you give feedback, receive feedback and outline how it benefits families.

1 Feedback begins with sharing difficult truths to family members in *honesty*, not in a spirit of *attack*. Therefore, you have to ask yourself, what is my intent when sharing the feedback? Do I want to build up my family member? Or do I want to tear them down? Being honest doesn't mean you sugarcoat the truth, but it also doesn't mean you beat someone over the head. Effective feedback strikes a balance between honesty and love.

2 In order to face uncomfortable truths given through feedback, you first have to be willing to *be vulnerable*, in the giving and receiving of feedback. It is an act of vulnerability to share some honest feedback without knowing how the other person will react. They may bite your head off or thank you. The truer the feedback, the harder it is to hear. When someone calls you out on your behavior and puts you in a really vulnerable spot, the first defense is to blame and experience anger. No one likes feeling vulnerable, but there's no way of benefitting from feedback otherwise.

Equally, it is an act of vulnerability to listen to someone's feedback without become defensive. If you listened to what they had to say, you are opening yourself up to potentially being hurt. But, by becoming defensive, you may also miss valuable information.

3 Be *vulnerable*. It takes courage to be vulnerable. Vulnerability happens when we drop our egos, stop trying to protect our pride, and really listen to what the other person has to say. Courage is the ability to face uncomfortable truths regarding yourself or your relationship. Yes, it is painful to face these things, but facing them empowers you to change. Courage is vital for healthy relationships. It is critical for working through a crisis. It is the grease that helps the wheels of change move. So don't let your ego get in the way of being vulnerable. As a result, when courageous and vulnerable, you are able to receive difficult but truthful feedback from another vulnerable person without damaging the relationship.

4 Pay attention to the impact of your words and actions. You may not have intended to hurt your son, daughter, wife, mother, father, grandparent, cousin, aunt, or uncle with your words or actions; but regardless of what you intended, hurt can still occur. You have to recognize that your words may have an effect that you may not have intended. Therefore, it is important to *pacify* a person's defensiveness before they have the chance to get defensive.

Begin your feedback by identifying strengths or struggles that are being seen in the other person. For example, "I appreciate how hard you've been working the last few weeks, yet there's something we need to discuss." Alternatively, you can acknowledge a struggle they've been challenged with lately: "I know work has been crazy for you the last few weeks and you haven't been sleeping well. I'd like to talk about something that's also been hard for me." This tool opens up the floor for feedback instead of defensiveness. It saves your family member from feeling like they're on the hot seat and it helps create a space for understanding and respectful and healthy confrontation.

How to Fight Fairly

Conflict is a natural aspect of any family. There's nothing unusual or unhealthy about conflict. In fact, it would be strange if a family didn't have conflict. Why? Conflict, in principle, can be a powerful thing. There is a strong functional purpose in conflict. Conflict allows for problems to be voiced and addressed, for feelings to be expressed, for negative behaviors to be challenged, and for family members to be held accountable. Conflict is not a battle to the death, it's a conversation aimed at resolution, reconciliation, and growth. Often, I see families carrying out conflicts poorly, leading to damaging and difficult results. To ensure the positive results of successful conflicts happen in your family, it's important to follow some basic rules

1 Don't play the "blame game." Assigning blame distracts you from finding solutions. When someone feels blamed, their entire attention is consumed by defending themselves or shifting the blame to something or someone else. This keeps both the accuser and the accused from focusing on solving the conflict at hand. Parents, you see this in your children when they are fighting – "Well, Susie hit me first!".

2 Throwing past failures in someone's face is not only irrelevant to the present, but designed only to hurt. Conflict should be navigated with the intent to bring about resolution and repair. But if your intent is to rack up points and inflict as much damage on others as possible, then you will never move forward. You also run the risk of damaging the relationship even more severely.

3 Verbal attacks like name-calling are unacceptable in conflict. Conflict ought to be something family members feel safe to engage in. It is the mechanism by which families seek resolution to their problems, not to wound the identity of the other party. If you name-call, you poison the well. You make what should be beneficial, as a tool, destructive and useless.

4 Dismissing the opinion or perspective of the person you are in conversation with is invalidating, and it will not serve you well. When people feel dismissed they tend to get out louder, more intense, and more defensive. This distracts from the goal of the conversation and everyone ends up dissatisfied and hurt. Dismissing the other person is simply unfair. Ask yourself, *if the other person did to me what I did to them, how would that make me feel?* If they dismissed you, you'd likely be upset, feeling disrespected and invalidated. So, why is it then acceptable for you to inflict that damage on someone else?

5 Just as with being dismissed, constant interruptions lead to louder, more intense, and more defensive conflict. This distracts from the resolution of the conflict. Again, ask yourself, *if the other person constantly* *cut me off midsentence and didn't let me finish my point, how would I feel?* You'd likely feel disrespected, invalidated, and frustrated. So, why is it acceptable for you to treat them in that manner when you demand respect from them?

When someone is expressing a view that you disagree with, it is important that you respond to what they *actually said* in its entirety. That is simply being respectful. If you selectively choose to respond to your assumptions about what they said or you respond to what they said only in part, it's damaging and will shut the door to resolving the situation. If you are being selective — cherry-picking the sticking points — that's an attempt to control and commandeer the conversation. It's only a way of misrepresenting the other person to fulfill your own agenda which is dangerous and a dead end.

Once more, ask yourself, *if the other person inaccurately cherry-picked what I said to fit their agenda, how would I feel?* You'd likely feel disrespected, invalidated, and frustrated. So, why is it acceptable for you to treat them in that manner when you demand respect from them?

How to De-escalate Heated Arguments

Escalated conversations are like runaway trains; the brakes are gone and the speed increases until something goes catastrophically wrong. When escalated, family members resort to their worst behavior. Loved ones say and do things that they regret afterwards. And the most dangerous aspect of escalated conversations is that we can't stop ourselves; the brakes are gone. We say and do what outlandish things to be heard, which backfires in the end. If this has been your experience with your family, don't lose hope. Change is possible, but it may come incrementally, this is *not* an immediate process. Here are three steps to initiate that incremental change.

1 The first incremental step towards change is to develop an awareness of how chemistry in our body shifts during these types of interactions. I've talked with many, many clients who told me about a regrettable argument of theirs, saying, "I couldn't recognize that things were getting escalated." The reason for this is that when the conversation becomes escalated, the emotional center of your brain essentially takes over. That leaves you at a disadvantage since the part of your brain that recognizes situational awareness goes offline. Instead of seeing a number of choices dictated by reason or values in response to the situation, you only see one of three options: flight, fight or freeze. This is precarious place to be in. Flight, fight or freeze are survival responses. They are extreme reactions and don't lend themselves to nuanced, intricate and patient work that sorting out family issues requires. Understanding what may be your "go-to" or default survival response in an escalated situation will serve you well. Knowing how you likely will respond and the shortfalls of that response, you can then plan ahead by envisioning scenario where, in an escalated situation, you respond with kindness, reason or patience.

2 Therefore, before an escalated argument ever occurs, you need to identify the *indicators* of an escalated argument. An easy metaphor would be the "check engine" light in the dashboard of your car. The whole point of that light is to let you know there's a problem and attention must be paid. I want you to ask yourself, *what are the indicators that alert me to the fact that an escalated argument is taking place?* Or, to add another angle to the question, what are indicators for my family member? It may be different. Some common indicators are: raised voices, aggressive body posture, insults and mockery, accusations, people talking over each other, or past mistakes being brought up. Identifying these indicators is crucial as eliminating them or changing them when they occurring could positively shift the conversation. Sometimes the most beneficial way of abolishing these signals is to call them out in real time. This can sound like someone saying "I notice that we're getting stuck in the habit of blaming" or "We're getting sucked into an unproductive conversation. I feel like neither of us are listening to the other." These are non-blaming, non-personalizing statements that orient everyone's attention to what's taking place.

You could even come up with a codename for the escalated pattern like "Tsunami" or "Whirlwind." These are fun, descriptive terms that, when stated, alert everyone to the presence of the pattern in a non-blaming way. Its less confrontative to say "Tsunami!" than to say "Well, your mom and her big mouth is at it again!"

3 Now that you've determined the indicators, your family can plan and enact a *strategy* for changing the direction of the escalated argument — a strategy that everyone agrees to follow. The strategy could consist of a time-out that everyone agrees to take when a family member says "Tsunami!" For some families, time-outs really work. For other families, time-outs don't work at all and may even escalate the situation more. In that case, they need to craft a different strategy where everyone stays in the conversation, but they all make a group effort to cool-off. Whatever your strategy is, having one is better than not. Without a strategy, out of control conversations will continue getting out of hand and will lead to the same, negative results. Additionally, the average outcome of family conversations will let you know if the strategy is working or needs adjusting.

| Family Story | The Suarez family were passionate when it came to their disagreements. They were great at sharing their thoughts and no one in the family was shy about stating what they thought. But, their passionate communication style often gave way to anger. Family members felt unheard and invalidated by the quick, escalated, and inattentive interactions. The family's response was for each member to get louder and repetitive so as to make their voice and

thoughts known. The conflicts would reach a fever pitch and never end well.

My first goal when working with the family was to slow the escalation pattern down, so as to allow the "heat" to cool and enable each person's reason to take control. Coaching the family, I advised the family, when fired up, to use HALT. HALT simply stands for Hungry, Angry, Lonely, Tired. The purpose is to help each individual identify an unmet emotional or physical need in the moment of conflict. If one or more of the needs have not been met, this could contribute to the intensity of their feelings.

One memorable evening, in the midst of a family escalation, I encouraged the middle son, Alex, to assess his needs using HALT. As he worked through each need, he realized he hadn't eaten since breakfast or consumed any water. Pausing the session for a short snack and drink break, the family and I resumed session. Alex was invited to identify a number on a scale of 1-10, 1 being in a Zen state and 10 being rage prior to the snack break. He replied with an 8. Asking the same question with the only change being his current number on the scale, he identified a 4. This decrease allowed him to sufficiently describe what lead up to the conflict, what his and other positions were, and why he was so upset. He was calm and avoid attacking or lashing out as he spoke. The remaining family members were then able to join the conversation and thus a productive conversation resulted quickly. When asked, the family expressed that this kind of productive conversation wouldn't occur when they were all fired up. For the Suarez family HALT worked well; after all, it cut Alex's intensity level in half.

The HALT skill is one among many. I've worked with many family who like being creative and coming up with their own version of HALT. Find a skill that works for your family and use it!

Chapter 6

Protective Family Factors

Maybe it feels like your family is out of the woods. The idea that the problem has resolved itself and there's nothing left to worry about. This is naïve thinking. The absence of a problem does not mean your family is problem-free. Challenges and struggles are par for the course and will continue to occur. Challenges and struggles should be anticipated by families, not avoided. These obstacles are opportunities for developing new ways of interacting. Also known as, protective family factors are new, healthy patterns of behavior that *guard against* toxic conflict, poor boundaries, disrespect, and unaddressed hurt and *promote* skills, mindsets, and habits that help families build resilience in the face of challenges.

How to Develop Growth Mindset for Families

Time and again, after suggesting some solution to a family, I've been met with the response, "We already know about that solution. We tried it. It doesn't work." But when asked *how* they tried the idea, families repeatedly complain that it just didn't deliver *immediate* and *dramatic* results. So Unsurprisingly, they quit. Discussion of their failed attempts generally then leads to my discovery of a problematic implementation of the skill. Typically, I find that families often only practice half of the skill, or employed it half-heartedly, or made one full attempt, but reverted to old habits once things got uncomfortable. Enter in my well-worn in response-the problem had nothing to do with the skill; the problem was how the family exercised the skill. If this is true of your family, I encourage you to consider three new ways of thinking.

1 Learn to accept the awkwardness of change as normal. Discomfort is not an indication that a skill isn't working or won't work. At the beginning, it can feel like learning to ride a bike. It can feel mechanical and forced. That's okay. You have to get through that uncomfortable period and keep working at it

— then and only then, will it feel natural. Have patience.

2 I had a professor in graduate school who once said, "There's no such thing as failure. There's only feedback."[5] Now, of course, there is such a thing as failure. The quote is meant to challenge the meaning you ascribe to failure. Does it help motivate your learning? Or, do you take it as a definitive and permanent state about how you can succeed? If you understand failure as a form of feedback on what doesn't work, failure then become incredibly invaluable. You know what doesn't work, which provides you with a better idea of what does. This works for individuals as well as for families. Families, through trial and error, grow in their understanding of how to better connect and relate to each other when they are attentive to the feedback of failure.

3 Failure is an inevitable aspect of change. It isn't a sign that things will never work out or that your plan isn't the right plan. Rather, allow yourself and your family members to anticipate the distress of collapse and to bravely embrace it. This is a growth mindset that successful families adopt. Change the meaning of failure in your life and encourage it as a positive instead of a negative. In failure are the seeds of growth.

---

[5] I owe this wisdom to Norm Thiesen, Ph.D.

| Family Story |

The Connors were a family who struggled with controlling their emotions. They would have awful, explosive fights and no one felt emotionally safe in the family. After reaching out and working with me, they realized they could have conversations without attacking and lashing out. I coached them through some hard topics and, to their credit, they made serious changes and progress. As their season in therapy was coming to a close, they hit a few bumps in the road. The family had come a long way, and yet they still doubted anything had really changed. They worried that when counseling finished, they would fall back into old habits.

They were right, if and only if, they forget to learn from their failures would they revert back to old habits. If they took their failures as feedback, they would continue to improve and grow. But, if they allowed failures to dictate their habits, then their worries would be valid. The family found reassurance in this response. The family went on to see failures, setbacks, and challenges as inspiration to promote growth.

How to Repair Relational Damage

Whenever there is toxic conflict within families that goes unresolved, damage to relationships is the natural progression. If the damage is not repaired, the relationship can become worse and even potentially deteriorate. Think of relational damage like a small crack in the foundation of a house. Given time, repeated harm, and even unforeseen external stressors, a small crack can grow to the point that the whole house can collapse. Therefore, it is paramount to identify the crack and repair it as soon as possible in order to save the house.

Relational damage from unresolved conflict doesn't just go away when the shouting stops. Ignoring it doesn't just make it disappear either. Pain and hurt are not soothed by silence, they flourish in it. Unresolved conflict leaves tension between family members that can result in additional conflict. Ironically, in trying so hard to avoid conflict, we create more of it. Relational damage must be repaired by those who created it if a relationship is to survive. Here's how.

1 This first step involves bringing your grievance to the other person's attention. Share with them how their behavior affected you. Be specific and concrete in your descriptions, but don't jump in with labels or judgments. Your goal is to be honest, not to attack. Think about how you would like someone to share a grievance with you. You likely would want someone to address with kindness. So, be willing to address your family members in the way you would like. Labels and judgments put the other person on the defensive and shuts down the communication process. The point in sharing is reconciliation and building awareness

2 After the wounded party addresses what happened and how it made them feel, it is the responsibility of the offender to acknowledge the negative effects of their actions. This can be hard, but acknowledgement is essential for repairing the relational damage. Just saying you're sorry does very little. Making an effort to understand the other person and verbally acknowledging their feelings is very healing. It allows for the foundation of trust to be built, which is essential for any meaningful relationship, in any family. If families were like the human body, trust would be the blood.

3 At this point, the two parties collaborate on what actions need to be taken to make an amends. The offender starts this process by asking, "What can I do to make things right between us?" The wounded party may have some ideas, or they may not and that's okay. Any suggestions for repairs should be expressed. This, ideally, should generate a number of ideas of which the offender can chose and commit themselves to the best one or more. And by committing to a new course of action, they are demonstrating a genuine desire for reconciliation that goes far deeper than mere words. For the injured party, let's be clear, this is *not* the time to lecture. This is a collaborative process between two people who both commit to healthy behaviors, attitudes, and mindsets. I encourage the injured party, when requesting specific changes — ask yourself, *in what ways can I support the other in their behaviors?* Change can only happen when you work together.

| Family Story |

The Chen family was stuck. From an outsider's view, they seemed to be a normal family with no major problems. But this was not the case. The Chen's oldest son, Samuel, made a series of bad choices when he was in adolescence that seriously wounded his family's trust and sense of safety in the home. Samuel felt bad for what he had done, attempting to hear out and understand his family's hurt. His poor choices changed him. He made a conscious effort to do better and be better, but this mattered little to his family. They could only see the "old" him, the version of him that wasn't safe.

When I started working with the family, I initially noticed that whenever the incident was mentioned, everyone shut down. I observed that no one knew how to discuss their hurt and pain. It was too scary. So, they avoided it. This resulted in continuous damage to the family relationships. Challenging them, I explored with the family the concept of "stuckness" which remains until they beginning sharing about what happened. The family lived in continuous pain, they were preventing Samuel's opportunity to make an amends. Coaching the family through steps 1-3, the family revisited their pain and hurt during Samuel's damaging behaviors and choices. Samuel responded by expressing true Samuel contrition and sorrow and was open to hearing how his family felt. He listened to their hurt, he acknowledged their feelings, and asked if there was anything he could do to make it right.

Hearing Samuel's response really surprised the family. Because they never had this kind of conversation, they never knew Samuel felt bad and wanted to restore the family trust. They hadn't bothered to inquire, and Samuel never felt safe enough to share. The family admitted that in many ways, Samuel already made the changes they wanted. Before this conversation, the family didn't feel like they could acknowledge Samuel's positive steps because they didn't trust his sincerity. Now they could.

How to Create and Maintain Respect

Building respect within a family begins with defining *respect* itself. Is it the way you communicate? Considering others before you speak or act? Does it have to do with attitude? These questions are important to settle. The answers circumscribe your accountability for your own behavior and what you are willing to tolerate from others. In the lived experience of many families, respect means honoring each other. It means hearing them out even when you disagree. It means being mindful of their needs, wishes and desires. It means considering how your choices and actions affect those around you. For you and your family, respect may mean these things and more. Talking with your family about what respect means to them is an important conversation to have for starting off on the right foot, or for recalibrating when a pattern of disrespect has developed. Below are four steps for creating a culture of respect in your family.

1 Model the behavior you wish to see in your spouse, child, sibling, or parent. It is not enough to demand respect from others when you are not behaving and speaking in the manner you are necessitating. It is not enough to demand something from another when you are not living up to your own standards. Behave in such a way that you wish others would behave towards you. And if members of your family do not behave in a respectful way, *do not let their behavior determine yours*. Be consistent with your own standards. If they will not respect you, have respect for yourself. Do not allow the disrespectfulness of their behavior to erode your own. Keep your standards intact regardless of the other person's behavior.

2 Sometimes people need to learn respect as a skill. Not everyone possesses the ability to respect themselves and others automatically. So then, your focus ought to be on how to teach, learn, and practice the skill rather than lashing out at those who lack it. This requires a shift in perspective. Reframing the disrespectful person's behavior will help you not take their actions personally. It will allow you to act compassionately towards them for the purpose of developing the skill of respect.

3 Be on the lookout for examples of respectful behavior. And when you do see it, even in tiny doses, praise it. Don't spend your time hyper-focusing on behaviors you dislike. Give most of your attention and energy to focusing on the behavior you want to see. This helps create a culture that values respect and affirms it when people behave respectfully.

4 On the other hand, know that acknowledging disrespect when it happens is sometimes necessary. Acknowledgement is not the same as lashing out or attacking. Whether you are a child or an adult, disrespect begets disrespect. In other words, disrespect, when responded to in kind, only leads to more disrespect. To head off the cycle, calmly express that the behavior is not acceptable and then move on.

Family Story Alice was a 74-year-old woman, enjoying her time in retirement. She liked getting together with friends, traveling, and was active in her local community. She was relatively healthy and financially secure. Alice had nothing but a charmed life except for one thing, Edward, her adult son. Edward would call his mom on a regular basis to curse and berate her for not sending him money or showing enough interest in him. Edward was used to getting his way with his mom and his most effective tool was disrespect. And Alice always felt powerless to do anything about it. She felt hurt by her son's behavior, but, worried that if she said anything, she'd disappoint her son and not fulfill her role of loving mother. This dynamic went on for some time with no change, when Edward hit a rough spot with finances and his health, and his belligerence towards his mother escalated, prompting Alice to seek counseling with me.

When we started working together, Alice shared how heartbroken she was every time her son would treat with such disrespect. She was a widow and didn't have a partner to lean on, so her relationship with her son was special to her. When he would treat her poorly she felt incredible hurt, but she didn't want to risk being a "bad mother" by challenging Edward's behavior. Challenging the idea that Alice is a bad mother if she confronts Edward's disrespectful behavior, I proposed, through sharing with her son that she will not tolerate disrespect from him, she is not harming him or their relationship. In fact, she is doing her son a favor. Alice could provide valuable feedback for her son and present him with an opportunity to learn what actual respect looks like. After all, she may be retired from her career, but she isn't retired from parenting. And the task before her is helping her son develop the skill of respect. She took a deep breath and said "Okay."

We outlined a plan involving the four steps described above. It took work. Alice had to change deeply ingrained habits and beliefs in herself, but over time, a new pattern of behavior emerged. Edward learned that his behavior was disrespectful and it didn't get him what he wanted. And when he wanted to blame his mom, he realized he didn't have a leg to stand on because, Alice was consistently respectful, but firm with him. He had no excuse for his appalling behavior. Over time, he became open to feedback from his mom and started making steps towards change.

How to Build Trust

Trust is very difficult to rebuild when broken, but rebuilding trust is not impossible. The two mistakes I have seen family members make many times over: a demand to be trusted immediately after breaking trust and cynicism toward the one trying to rebuild trust. In order to restore broken trust, appropriately, families must follow a structure. How do we strike that balance?

1 In order to reestablish trust, it is important to discuss expectations that everyone will honor. Identify the reason that trust was broken in the first place. Was it an expectation not being respected? Was it an unreasonable expectation being strictly enforced? Was it an expectation that was articulated unclearly? So, go back to the drawing board: have everyone explain the expectations they have of each other. Be open to the feedback of family members who push back on your expectations and listen to the reasons why they are unhappy with them. Use the negotiation skills discussed earlier in the book to agree upon fair and clear expectations that allow everyone to be on board with. Have patience with each other because this conversation takes some time and can be painful and uncomfortable.

2 After you've established your expectations of each other, be consistent. You may have a perfectly fair expectation for your family, however, if you are not consistent in how you apply and enforce it, they will have just cause to accuse you of being unfair. Inconsistency comes with a cost. And if you try to backtrack or explain away your inconsistency, you are in danger of being purposefully unclear. Either way, that kind of behavior undermines trust.

You must also be consistent in how you observe the expectations of others. If you are inconsistent in how you respect the expectations of others, you will rightly be accused of maintaining a double-standard.

Inconsistency undermines trust. Confusion, double-standards, backtracking, and inconsistency are all trust-killers. So be consistent, even when it's inconvenient or uncomfortable. After trial and error, be willing to revisit the expectations conversation feedback within the family When each family member can assure safety to each other that feelings can be honestly shared, a major step is taken towards rebuilding trust.

3 *Trust is incrementally restored over time.* Trust has more to do with character than anything else. And since character is forged and proven over time, time is necessary for trust to be restored. Trust should be given when there is evidence of trustworthiness, not the promise of trustworthiness. Again, this comes down to character, not words.

I define *character* as intentions demonstrated through behavior over the course of time. For example, if a husband has been unfaithful to his wife, but then tells her his infidelity was a mistake and he truly is committed to her — should she believe him? I would recommend that she reserve judgment. She should wait to see what he does over the course of time. If her husband makes statements of commitment but doesn't stop cheating on his wife, she has no grounds for trust in him. But if after making those statements, the husband, for several years following, stays faithful to his wife, then she has grounds for trusting him. She trusts him based on his behavior — based on the evidence of his fidelity borne out over time — not merely on his promise of fidelity. If I were to work with this couple, I would advise the husband as follows: if you have a good intention, then your behavior will give evidence of it by repeated example. Let character be the foundation of trust.

How to Form and Maintain Boundaries

Healthy boundaries are foundational to any healthy relationship. Personal boundaries help cultivate a sustainable connection between two people. Without boundaries, people will cross lines they shouldn't, and relationships will ultimately deteriorate. But it's irrelevant to talk about the importance of *boundaries* unless we know what they are. Boundaries are consistent standards of acceptable and unacceptable behavior. An obvious and generalized example of such would be that I don't give out my social security number to strangers. But a relational boundary, addresses the idea that we can emotionally set standards as well. Common examples of such would be requesting that your friends don't gossip or making it clear that a nickname you hate should not be used.e

Problems occur when boundaries have not been clearly established. People will take advantage of you or accuse you of holding inconsistent standards when boundaries have not been established. Furthermore, I've heard it said — and I think it's true — that if you do not define your boundaries, someone else will do it for you. Someone else's boundaries, which may not be to your benefit, will be imposed upon you leading to potentially painful feelings or reactions. Let's look at some steps to setting, enforcing, and respecting your own boundaries and those of others.

1 Define your boundaries. Ask yourself, *what is acceptable behavior regarding how someone interacts with me?* You have the right to define what is acceptable and unacceptable. That isn't a guarantee that people will always act in the manner you wish them to, but knowing your boundaries makes you aware of when people are, or are not, respecting them. Then, define unacceptable behavior. Ask yourself, *Is it okay for someone to insult me? Is it okay for someone to curse at me? Is it okay for someone to lie to me?* These important questions help you think through the limits of what you are willing to tolerate from others.

2 Defining boundaries is a fantastic first step, but defined boundaries are useless if you do not consistently enforce them. "Enforce" can be a scary word; let me explain what I mean. I do not mean to say that you strong-arm people into abiding by your standards. You are not a "Boundaries Law Enforcement Officer." What I mean by enforcing your boundaries is that when someone violates one, you don't ignore it. You state to the other person that what they did violated your boundary, and that their behavior is unacceptable. Don't be rude or disrespectful in the way you enforce a boundary, just simple address the violation. And do it consistently. Inconsistent enforcement of boundaries can do just as much damage to relationships as undefined boundaries.

There's no guarantee that others will respect your boundaries, but if you enforce one, you raise the likelihood for respect which lead to healthier relationships. And if there's someone in your life who refuses to respect your boundaries, you need to ask yourself if that person is worth keeping in your life — or at least in a close, intimate way. Not respecting someone's boundaries is a clear demonstration of disrespect or lack of regard and they may not be the most emotionally safe people in our lives.

3 The final step in this process is to consistently respect the boundaries of others. If you do not observe and respect the boundaries of others, what reason do others have for observing and respecting your own? By not respecting others' boundaries, you shoot yourself in the foot and can potentially harm the relationships you have with others and, ultimately, yourself. When you ignore the boundaries set by others, you ignore the connection you have with them. Sending a clear message that you don't care about them and what they mean to you.

It's also important to remember that boundaries are not bargaining chips. They are not to be "wheeled and dealed" to get what you want out of relationships, nor should they be used as bait for change. Boundaries are not "If you (fill in the blank), then I'll (fill in the blank)." They go hand in hand with respect and if you eliminate the respect you have for others and even yourself when making boundaries, you aren't really creating boundaries. You are creating threats.[6]

> **Family Story** Maggie and Craig were devoted parents. They both worked hard and made a decent income. They had two kids close in age, a boy and girl. When their two kids entered high school, the couple felt the desire to adopt. Nervous about the idea, the couple decided to move forward with their plan believing it was the right choice given the need

---

[6] I have Samantha Cunningham, LMHC to thanks for this bit of wisdom.

in their community. They adopted an adolescent boy, Max who came from a string of chaotic foster homes.

At first, the family was excited to have Max. However, problems quickly emerged. Max struggled with following the schedule of the family. He wanted to go to bed when he wanted. He wanted to eat what he wanted. He didn't complete the chores given to him. These small conflicts escalated to a serious stalemate. As much as they tried, nothing was changing so they reached out for help.

I started working with the family and realized that Max was smart enough to know what was expected from him and why, but he didn't feel secure in the family so he tested boundaries. This demonstrated a need for the family to discuss how to define, enforce, and respect boundaries with Max. Until that point, Maggie and Craig just assumed boundaries common to most family would be obvious to Max. But for Max, he never experienced healthy boundaries with a family, ever. So, along with the family, I walked them through boundary formation and maintenance with Max. This conversation allowed everyone to get on the same page. Maggie and Craig were able to explain to Max what boundaries were and why they are important. Max not only gained understanding, but also felt included in the family. Thereafter, the family worked their hardest to respect the boundaries expressed, and experienced better relationships with each other than they had previously.

How to Problem-Solve

Problem-solving is a collaborative effort done between family members with the goal of identifying problems and solutions. Problem-solving is a process. It must be done carefully; otherwise good ideas can be missed and great solutions never discovered. But to get *to* the good ideas, everyone must feel *safe* enough to share their ideas, good or bad. Below I've outlined with you the process families I've worked with have found most beneficial.

1 Identify the problem. Be sure to describe the problem in concrete and behavioral terms. Do not make the problem personal. Assigning blame is counterproductive and will often lead to other problems. Personalizing the problem can make a person feel attacked, which leads to defensiveness, and then the whole conversation is likely to turn into a fight. Since you've probably done plenty of that already, a different kind of conversation is necessary. Describe *what* the problem is, not *who* the problem is. Here are a few examples: "It is a problem when commitments aren't followed through", "It doesn't work when chores aren't completed by the agreed time", "Screaming and yelling don't let us communicate effectively." These are far more effective uses of language, as they allow everyone to interact with the problem.

2 Brainstorm solutions. There is no such thing as a bad idea ... well, maybe there is — but at least during the brainstorming step, you should come up with as many ideas as you can, regardless of whether they at first seem good, mediocre, or just plain bad. The point of this step is to get creative, to think outside the box. Sometimes the idea that no one had considered at first is the best idea. It is important to not critique or mock one another for sharing their ideas. Make sure everyone feels safe and comfortable to share. Sometimes it takes coming up with three or four or five bad or mediocre solutions to find to a good one. Simply put, you might have brainstorm and implement the changes multiple times before you see the solution that works the best.

3 Weigh the pros and cons of each solution, and eliminate the worst. Nail down the best ideas and come up with a short list of possible solutions for the problem. At this stage, using healthy communication skills is vital. You will have to give clear, reasonable explanations why an idea is or isn't good. Be prepared to explain your position with specifics. Don't just shoot down ideas because you don't like them furthermore don't just demand that everyone follow your idea without a thoughtful rationale. Explanation may lead to negotiation. Make sure to interpret negotiation as the process of family members getting onboard with your idea.

4 Choose the best idea from your short list, and then make a plan. Make sure your plan is *practical*, is marked by *attainable goals*, and is *assessable*. Your plan has to be simple enough that everyone can take action on it. If it's too complicated or dependent on future circumstances, then your plan isn't practical. Give a timeline for when you will start, when you will assess the effectiveness of the plan, and by what time you hope to complete the stated goals. If the plan is vague, then there's no way of telling if you are making progress or not. Make your plan concrete with obvious ways to judge progress. And be sure to find supporters who can keep you accountable or encourage you along the way. The biggest mistake people make when trying something new is to think they can do it alone. You are at your strongest when you have the support of others.

5 Review the effectiveness of your solutions and plan. It is okay to admit when a plan isn't working: admitting struggle isn't a sign of failure. It merely allows you the opportunity to formulate a new, better plan based on additional information of what doesn't work. Remember that sometimes to get to the best solution, you have had to try others that didn't work. Furthermore, it is very helpful for family members to give each other feedback during this process. Feedback is necessary for growth and resolution of the problem. Make use of the feedback-giving skills you learned in the previous section.

Fetu and Lelei moved to the United States when they were a young couple. They bought a home, started their careers and family. They raised their kids in traditional Samoan culture. And for many years, the family was happy with little issues. However, when their oldest son, William, entered into high school, he started rebelling against his parents. The family fought bitterly over issues ranging from the son's clothing, cleanliness of his room, his interests in music, and the type of friends he had. William felt like he had no say in his family. He felt like he was expected to conform to what his family's expectations and if he didn't like it, that was his problem.

Their conflicts over the next few years increased in frequency and intensity to the point that family members didn't feel safe at home. They sought out counseling get help. When I started working with them, I discovered the conflicts usually regarded William asserting his preferences and will in the home. Parents viewed this as a threat to their authority. I suggested to the family steps 1-5 of problem-solving techniques discussed above. The family attempted to work on their unhealthy conversations. The steps provided a way for everyone to collaboratively work through divisive issues, something everyone desperately wanted. The conclusion — it helped the family see the problem as a problem and not as a person. This drained the emotional intensity out of the conversation allowing everyone to be more calm and rational as they discussed the issue. This was a major win-win for everyone.

How to Cultivate Connection

Constant focus on problems can be a problem in and of itself. There needs to be balance in a family's focus. If the problem always controls everyone's attention, then you run the risk of burning relationships out. If your only point of contact with each other is the problem, you need to cultivate a positive connection outside of the problem. Connecting over something positive gives everyone a breather and provides a level of confidence in that even though there are problems, we still have a safe connection with each other. Here's how to do that.

1 Connect over interests. Notice that I don't say to connect over *common* interests. Connecting over common interests is usually the basis for friendship, but familial relationships tend to be deeper than friendships. Family members need to show curiosity in the interests of other family members. This is key to relational health. Whether the interests of your family member align with your own is irrelevant. If you care about your family members, you will take an interest in their interests.

2 Plan and do fun activities together that everyone enjoys. That can be a tough task when everyone only agrees to disagree on what is fun. The goal here is for everyone to stay flexible. Sacrifice for attaining the bigger goal of connecting with your family members is a must. The art of negotiation also should be present in these conversations. No single person should be only one choosing every activity.

3 Establish regular family activities that everyone can participate in like a regular family dinner, movie night, game night, church attendance, or bowling — the sort of thing everyone can participate in. This creates a space where the family can just enjoy one another and be purposeful about spending time with each other. Set sensible rules that everyone can agree on like no phones or friends. Everyone will protect the time for the family.

Simeon was a hurting, troubled

| Family Story | 16-year-old who recently lost his grandpa. The loss of his grandpa was unlike any other feeling as he practically raised Simeon. Having nowhere else to go, the young man moved in with his estranged dad, Jack. Simeon and his dad had not spoken to each other in years and their reunion was awkward to say the least. Simeon believed for years that his dad abandoned him which led to Simeon feeling resentment and bitterness towards him. For his dad, it was a rough transition too. He had limited parenting experience with his son and didn't quite know how to handle a teenager. Jack tried enforcing rules and expectations, but Simeon rebelled against each one. The family was in a dire place when they reached out for counseling.

When we started working together, it became evident to me that Jack and Simeon had no relationship. They had no connection. It was easy to see why Jack's effort to enforce rules and expectations (an appropriate thing to do for a parent of a teenager) utterly failed with Simeon. The bond, the connection, the trust that develops over time, through the relationship, was not there. So, coaching the two of them, they worked to build a positive connection prior to having the difficult conversations about rules and expectations. The two of them recognized that they needed a positive relational foundation before they started adding rules and expectations to their relationship. Forming a solid relational connection sets the foundation for ongoing dialogue. Teens are more likely to respect the rules when they feel like they have a say.

In session, we began discussing common interests and other topics of interest. I coached them on how to show interest in the other person even if they didn't share the same passion. Then they progressed to the point of planning fun things to do together so as to create shared positive memories and experiences. They then established family routine activities that gave them ways to connect on a regular basis. Over time, the two built a good and healthy relationship, which made the difficult conversation about rules and expectations far easier. They both felt a degree of trust that was not present before. Their investment in the relationship diffused future conflicts, enabled them to have difficult conversations, and created a positive regard towards each other, which lead to healthy development in their relationship.

Chapter 7

Changing Dysfunctional Family Roles

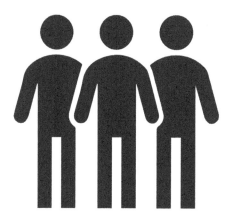

If you've ever watched kids on a playground, you know exactly how enthusiastic kids can get when playing games. You also have probably noticed how enthusiastic kids can get for the rules of the game, which can be comical since children aren't terribly coordinated, knowledgeable of the rules or adept at executing the strategies of a particular games. Over the course of a game, more time is spent arguing about the rules than playing the actual game. It's especially comical when kids try acting out different roles (or positions) on their respective teams. For example, when playing basketball, the player giving the inbound pass at the baseline becomes confused since her four other players are holding their hands up saying their open to take the ball down the court. There can't be four point guards! There are 5 players on a basketball team, and each player has their own role. Roles provide order to chaos. But all roles were not created without problems. Roles can have problems: a player can misunderstand their role; a player can act out a role for an entirely different sport; a player can act out a role that is self-serving rather than benefitting their team. Roles can have the appearance of providing order to chaos, while in fact, perpetuating the chaos. This is a rather benign problem when contained to the playground, but for families, this problem can have catastrophic effects.

As it relates to families, roles can present hidden obstacles prevent your family's progress. What is that hidden obstacle? It is dysfunctional family roles that perpetuate the toxic pattern of behavior. Dysfunctional family roles unconsciously influence the behavior and responses of individuals. Family roles and toxic patterns of behavior go hand in hand because toxic patterns of behavior influence individuals in the family to "play out" dysfunctional roles. Vice versa, dysfunctional family roles enable the toxic pattern of behavior to continue. In order to get out of this crisis and see change in your family, the dysfunctional family roles everyone "plays" must change as well as the toxic pattern of behavior.

There are five roles that people typically play in dysfunctional families and all five roles work together to hide and distract from the distress in the family that the members are afraid or unwilling to address. In some families, members may play multiple roles or may even transition from one role to another circumstances and dynamics shift. The roles, on a conscious level, may not seem dysfunctional or unhealthy. A family member may even state that they act out their role to help the family. Yet, when analyzing how these roles affect the family from an objective, big picture point of view, it is evident that they only perpetuate dysfunctional as you will see throughout this chapter. Identifying what they are and how they enable the toxic pattern of behavior that takes place in your family opens up your family to experiencing healing from distress and connected relationships.

1 **The Hero**: The hero role is played by someone in the family who, despite the family struggles, has risen above the chaos. Think of Luke Skywalker from *Star Wars*. The Skywalker family produced the greatest villain the cosmos has ever seen, Darth Vader, but at least the Skywalkers have Luke to look up to. The hero is someone on whom the family pins their hopes, dreams, and aspirations. If the hero can make it in the world, then their family isn't all that bad. If something goes right, it's the hero's doing. The hero can rescue the family from the problem or distract them from it. However, if the family experiences distress due to their unaddressed dysfunction, the sentiment can quickly turn against the hero. The hero can be transformed into another role, the scapegoat, which will be described later. The family may blame the hero for failing them.

How does this dysfunctional role perpetuate the toxic pattern of behavior in the family? The hero has a way of making the family feel good. There's nothing wrong with feeling good, there's nothing wrong with looking up to certain family members, and there's nothing wrong with being proud of a family member. Yet, you must understand, feeling all those things just mentioned should never come at the cost of paying attention to your family issues. The hero should not be a distraction to addressing the family issues — but the person playing the hero often takes this on themselves and the family equally pressures them to take full responsibility. Sometimes it is appropriate for the family to feel all of the negative emotions that come with the family distress.

People don't change when they are comfortable. The anxiety, pain, hurt, and frustration that feels inescapable is in fact helpful and creates change, it just makes everyone uncomfortable. Discomfort is what challenges the *status quo* and motivates people to change.

The Scapegoat: This family member gets blamed for all that's wrong with the family. Think of Simba from the *Lion King*. It was Scar's plot to kill his brother, Mufasa, to take the throne. In order for his plan to work without creating suspicion, he created a situation where Simba was the scapegoat for his father's death. If something goes wrong, it's automatically assumed to be the scapegoat's fault. Someone playing this role allows the family to focus blame on one person and away from a pattern of behavior. This focus acts as a pressure valve, allowing for the family to vent all their feelings that have been building up.

How does this dysfunctional role perpetuate the toxic pattern of behavior in the family? If all credit for the family's successes goes to the hero, then all blame for the family's struggles goes to the scapegoat. This is the person whom the family sees as "the problem." A common example of this is when families have one child who is very well-behaved and another child who is struggling behaviorally. They are the one who have made everyone else miserable. Everything would be fine if the scapegoat wasn't the way they are.

Not always, but often enough, families start their counseling by giving me a line like, "If only [name of scapegoat] hadn't …everything would be good." When pressed, it becomes evident that the issues they are dealing with aren't limited to the scapegoat, but the scapegoat serves as a useful pressure valve through whom the family can direct all their frustrations. Just like with the hero, the scapegoat becomes a distraction from the real problem.

3 **The Symptom-Bearer**: This family member is sensitive to all the stress, hurt, and emotional damage in the family. Think of Elsa from the movie *Frozen*. She felt thought she was a burden to her family, so she tried suppressing her powers. Her fear turned to anxiety and social isolation as she hid herself away in her room, year after year. Some dysfunctional families may not openly speak about their issues, but the effects of their issues can be manifestly seen in the symptom-bearer. Often the person who plays this role is physically sick, or has psychosomatic disorders, or struggles with addiction, or all of the above.

How does this dysfunctional role perpetuate the toxic pattern of behavior in the family? There are several ways in which the symptom-bearer can distract everyone from addressing the real problem and perpetuate the toxic pattern of behavior, but these are often subtler than what happens with the hero or scapegoat. Let's say someone in the family points out what isn't working, actually giving voice to the problems in the family. The symptom-bearer is sensitive to whatever discomfort the family feels in the situation and will manifest that stress and anxiety physically or psychologically. So then, the response of the family might be to silence the person who is giving voice to the problem out of a concern for the symptom-bearer. Stated another way, family members may feel protective of the symptom-bearer and suppress discussion of the problem so as not to upset or harm her or him.

How often have we heard, "Shh! We don't need to talk about that with Grandma. It will just make her sick."

The symptom-bearer can also distract the family from addressing the toxic pattern of behavior by inadvertently focusing all of the family's attention on themselves. They may need intensive medical or mental health care, perhaps requiring regular doctor, hospital, or psychiatric appointments. Treatment may be very time-consuming and expensive, so the family has to rearrange their schedules around the symptom-bearer. Having to give that level of care consumes the family's time, energy, and focus, which doesn't allow the big issues to be addressed.

4 The Lost One: The lost one is emotionally or physically distant from the family. Think of Adaline Bowman from the movie *The Age of Adaline*. She was an immortal woman trying to live a normal life, but in order to main the façade of normalcy so as to not become a science experiment, she had to blend in and direct as little attention to herself as possible. The lost one makes their best effort to be unseen and unheard. They often blame the family's dysfunction on themselves, much like the symptom-bearer, and in an attempt to help, they remove or avoid drawing attention to themselves.

How does this dysfunctional role perpetuate the toxic pattern of behavior in the family? The lost one can be described as a wallflower. In other words, avoidant of conflict or addressing the family's issues, they do not want to be seen or heard. They are the ones who shut down or run away if they get any hint of the toxic pattern of behavior. This is problematic in that much needed conflict never occurs. Some conflict is necessary for the problem to be addressed, in the open, with everyone involved, in order for change to occur. But because of the lost one's reticence over the problem, the problem remains unaddressed. Alternatively, the lost one may just leave the family completely, without providing any context about why they left. This leaves the family in confusion; family members may blame themselves and feel guilty on an individual level and become even further distracted from the real problem. Or instead, they may get angry as they sit in the dark over the reasons the lost one left which further justifies that the problem is not the family, but one person. The family is distracted; their anger keeps them from identifying and addressing the real problem.

The Court Jester: This family member is a performer. Think of Tigger from *Winnie the Pooh*. Tigger is the relentless attention-seeking optimist. He loves being the center of attention. And he has a way of putting a lighthearted spin on every situation, even at times when the hundred-acre forest is faced with a threat. The court jester's role is to distract the family from the gravity of what's going on by making light of it, by turning the family drama into a form of entertainment — or even by creating new drama out of thin air. When there has been a big upset, the court jester makes everyone feel better by breaking the tension, which helps everyone forget what just happened.

How does this dysfunctional role perpetuate the toxic pattern of behavior in the family? Whenever the toxic pattern of behavior rears its ugly head, the court jester will jump into action. They will try to put a positive or humorous spin on what just happened to distract from it. Or they can create some kind of drama, external to the family, that sucks everyone in. They bring in a conflict from school, or with a boyfriend or girlfriend; maybe their coach is against them, or a teacher at school has it out for them, or the boss at work is a bully. Whatever the flavor of external drama, it acts as a light distraction for everyone in the family, taking them away from their pain, hurt, or anger. In a way, it's like the court jester creates an enemy, external to the family, whom everyone bonds together against.

Truthfully, there's nothing wrong with humor or trying to find the positive in a bad situation. Sometimes everyone needs a break from their problems and the hard work of solving them and there are other times when a teacher or coach or boss legitimately has it out for someone — and it is entirely appropriate for the family to rally around the family member who is being attacked. However, if humor, positivity, or external drama is your default move whenever the family problem manifests itself, that will only distract from the core issue.

Typically, members of a family only one or two of the roles listed above. However, family members can also play multiple roles, simultaneously. I once worked with a family where all the dysfunctional family roles were in play. I'm not kidding. Here's the story.

Ed, a physically abusive father was also, ironically, the court jester. In order to lighten the mood after he lashed out physically at his family, he shared funny stories, cracked jokes, and tried to pass his abuse off as if it were a joke. Consequently, the oldest son, Jared, was the hero. He moved out of the home. He went to college, got good grades, and worked a successful job. His achievements were often the focal point of family discussions. Ed would often say that his behavior "couldn't be *that* bad" since Jared was doing so well. The successes of Jared *must* make everyone feel good. The youngest son, Johnathan, received all the blame for the family problems. He was the scapegoat. The way Dad would put it, Johnathan *forced* him to lash out in anger because his behavior was so disrespectful. Melody, the mom, was the symptom-bearer. She felt paralyzed by her husband's reign of terror over the family and she wanted to protect Johnathan, but she didn't know how. All the pain and stress manifested in her life as an anxiety disorder. Even though she was on medication, it didn't help. She wouldn't leave the house or her room for days on end. In this way, she played a second role, the lost one, as well.

Family Story

Collectively, everyone was terrified to discuss what was really going on. If the outside world knew what went on in their home, it would be incredibly shameful and embarrassing. Individually, everyone had the intention of making the problem better, but unwise and unhealthy actions led to the perpetuation of the problem regardless of good intentions.

As I said before, toxic patterns of behavior in families are shameful and secretive; they are self-perpetuating and force people into dysfunctional roles to maintain the family's dignity. But if your family is caught in a destructive pattern, there is hope. Change is possible. It's been said that "you are as sick as your secrets."[7] The secrets you keep as a family have the potential to suffocate each member's emotional health. Breaking the silence and facing what's really going on is only the path forward. Here are six steps to change the dysfunctional effects of the five family roles.

1 Break free from individual blame and look at how the whole family participates in the problem. Look at the role *you* play and how it contributes to the problem. "No one is to blame, but everyone is responsible"[8] is a guiding axiom that perfectly the point.[9]

---

[7] A common saying uttered at Alcoholic Anonymous meetings and a paraphrase from *Alcoholics Anonymous: The Big Book.*

[8] I owe this wisdom to Kerri Duke, LSW.

[9] This guiding axiom is generally true, for most families. However, in cases of domestic violence and abuse, the victim is not the one to blame. The abuser needs to take responsibility for their actions in order for the family to grow. Please see *Appendix A* for more information about domestic violence and abuse.

2 What can you do differently to counteract the role you play and how it perpetuates the problem? For example, if you typically play the role of Court Jester, take a step back from making a joke or sharing an entertaining story and look at how your behavior distracts everyone from the problem. Whatever role you play, ask yourself how it's bolstering the unhealthy family dynamic and give it some serious thought. Seeing how your role perpetuates dysfunction in the family will empower you to make choices that address the problem and lead towards change.

3 Don't let shame keep you in silence.[10] Is maintaining the secret worth perpetuating the pain? Denial keeps your family stuck. You must *name the problem* in order to address it. You need to define it, out loud, in the presence of your family members. Yes, that will be uncomfortable, even scary. But an unnamed problem is an unchangeable one.

4 You cannot change another person, but you can change *you*. By refusing to go along with the toxic pattern of behavior or to play out your dysfunctional family role, you force change. Remember, the family is an interconnected system. If one part in the system starts acting differently, that has an effect on the

---

[10] If you are in a domestic violence and abuse situation, you may want to use caution in how you make your voice heard. You may need to seek out safety and support before you confront your abuser. Please seen *Appendix A* for more information regarding domestic violence and abuse.

whole. Imagine the ripples in a pond when a stone is dropped in, the pond is influenced by the change in the water. This is the idea of creating change for yourself.

5 Family systems are like government bureaucracies. They can be slow and resistant to change. So be patient and give it time. If you decide to break away from the unhealthy family status quo, expect resistance. People don't like change and your family will want you to act in the ways you always have. Despite the pushback, be consistent in healthy ways of living. You will be tempted to fall back into old patterns, but don't give in. Change will come.

6 Family roles, in and of themselves, are not dysfunctional. Some families flexibly switch back and forth between positive roles like being the supporter, the communicator, the leader, the teammate, the partner, the helper, or the collaborator. It may not be enough to simply eradicate the 5 dysfunctional roles from your family to ensure lasting change. The absence of a dysfunctional family role is like a black hole and will suck any life into it. You will need to substitute the dysfunctional role for a healthy, functional alternative. I suggest you get creative and think of, as a family, what kinds of roles you play with each other that are positive and life-giving.

These five roles are to dysfunctional families like water to a fish. The dysfunction has been going on for so long it has become common place and unnoticeable. You've learned to tolerate dysfunction. That's why it is important to step away from your family and look at it from an outsider's perspective. Objectively examine behaviors, responses, roles, and patterns of behaviors. Seeing your family from the outside gives you fresh eyes to notice where problems are and where potential solutions lie. It also helps you understand how you contribute to the problem and what you can do to change. I recommend everyone in the family do this. But even if some members aren't is willing, individuals can still make a big difference in changing dysfunctional family systems.

Chapter 8

Setbacks and Goals

Falling into old habits, backtracking, taking two steps forward with three steps back — or whatever else you want to call it — are a normal part of change. The reason-- change is hard. It is hard to try something new. It is hard to change a habit. Setbacks are a part of change, not the opposite of change. They are not just a possibility, but a *probability*. Therefore, give yourself and each other some grace. Don't expect perfection. Instead, look for small (or even large) glimpses of progress.

But how do you know when you are making progress? I've worked with many families who work hard, yet have no method of determining success. In order to observe change in your family, you need to create a plan. And not any ol' plan. A plan crafted in such a way that it has the highest probability of succeeding. When you do encounter setbacks, you must think of them as an aid to this created plan.

The worst thing you can do in the face of a setback is to "throw the baby out with the bath water." Don't disregard the positive steps you've put forward when setbacks occur. You have been living with the problem for so long already, you also must allow change the time to take root. Don't expect it to come immediately. Adjust your expectations and be realistic.

Setbacks can also be the back door to future success. What do I mean by that? Remember my professor's quote from the last chapter: "There's no such thing as failure. There's only feedback." Setbacks work in the same way. Setbacks, when you've reflected on and learned from them, can make your efforts even more effective. Here are three steps to get every ounce of benefit out of your setbacks.

1 Form good goals and smart plans. You may be encountering a setback simply because your goals and plans aren't as strong as they could be. When families start to recognize all the changes they need to make, it can be overwhelming. Feeling overwhelmed doesn't help with motivation. The solution isn't to work harder, but smarter. Sustainable change is supported by goals and a plan to accomplish those goals. Every family needs goals, but not every goal or plan is created equal. Some goals and plans are indeed better than others. Don't make the mistake of thinking change isn't possible when what you planned falls through. It is possible. Your goals may just be too ambitious — impractical, unrealistic, or even not as thought out as needed. If so, don't give up on goal-making. Go back to the drawing board and try the process again, instead, following a few suggestions to increase the likelihood that your goal will be successfully achieved.

Ask yourself, *what aspect of our family needs to change?* Better communication? Better conflict resolution? Better time management? Determine where the problems are and where you need to grow as a family. In one sentence, describe what you want. This statement will serve as your goal.

The trick during this stage is to be specific with how you are going to achieve your goal. I call these *objectives*. Objectives are the way you are going to accomplish the goal. Let's say, for example, you want your family to communicate better. Great — but if that's as clearly as you can articulate your goal, you won't get very far. You need to set *concrete*, *behavioral*, *measurable* objectives on how you are going to accomplish the goal. *How* are you going to communicate better as a family? Answer that question. "We will practice deep breathing before speaking. We will use a minimum of five *I*-statements during the conversation. We will take

115

a time-out when the conflict becomes escalated and then come back to conversation when calm." These are concrete, behavioral, and measurable objectives that will help you keep accountable to your goal and plan. The *how* allows for a goal to become possible and understandable to the whole family without assumptions.

Don't be afraid to make your objectives literally *quantifiable.* Pursuing a vague goal with a vague objective is like driving in thick fog. You think you're going the right way, but you have no clue if you're making progress because you can't see. Numbers help clear the fog so to speak. What if your family's objective was to listen better? What does that mean specifically? What if family members felt like they were listening better, but the conversation still became escalated and lead to results no one wanted? It would be impossible to determine if "better listening" really did or did not happen without concrete, behavioral, measurable targets set by the family. Let's break down how this works. If a family is introduced to the skill of practicing *I*-statements, progress might be considered as using only one *I*-statement. Initially, one is better than none, but you'd better see that number increase if you want to make progress towards your goal of better communication. Maybe you see progress after using two or three or even four *I*-statements. As you start getting better outcomes, you know will be able to directly link *I*-statements to the positive change. If you are increasing your use of

I-statements and better outcomes aren't seen, then you know you need to focus your attention on a different communication skill or use *I*-statements in combination with another communication skill.

CIn order to accomplish a goal, the objective must be within *your* control. What do I mean by that? Changing another person *is not* within your control; however, changing how *you* respond to that person *is*. So don't make your goal dependent upon another person or situation changing. That simply leaves you stuck. Divide what you want into two categories: what is *within* your control and what is *outside* your control. Once you've done that, create attainable and measurable objectives for what is within your control, and accept what is outside your control. For example, a family wants to communicate more effectively, so everyone commits to practicing the "I" Statement skill. Everyone is responsible to practice the skill regardless of what others are doing. Ideally, everyone would be practicing the skill in unison, without mistakes. Reality is usually messier. Mistakes will be made. A family member may not be fully motivated yet. That's okay. It doesn't have to be perfect. Don't make your commitment to practice the skill based on another's behavior.

D*Evaluate* whether your actions are successful or unsuccessful, getting you closer or farther away from your goal. Evaluation is a meaningful way to measure progress. In order to do this, you need to ask yourself, *are your efforts effective?* Is what you're doing getting you the results you want? If so, then keep going. If not, it's time to make adjustments. Adjustments are a normal part of pursuing a goal. Evaluation is a rather simple step, but there are some complexities to consider. You will need to determine if your goal and plan are getting you the results you want. Or, if the problem lies not with the goal, but how you are executing the goal. For example, a family that commits to using "I" Statements may not see success because they are practicing the skill poorly. In response to the poor results, they toss out a perfectly good skill that could actually help them if used properly. This is a major problem for a number of reasons. First, by tossing out the skill they lose the potential benefit the skill would provide if used properly. Second, by not being aware of their improper use of the skill, it may be likely that the next skill they chose to practice will also be used improperly. Unknowingly, they set themselves up for failure by having no means to evaluate adeptness at using skills. Third, they run the risk of losing hope and motivation. Patience can only last for so long. Having tried and failed reduces the likelihood of families ever taking the risk again. And fourth, they waste valuable time. Time is valuable and finite resource. In a serious crisis, a skill working or not in window of time can mean the difference of a family staying together or falling apart. Therefore, given the particulars of a family crisis, families need to be effective with the motivation and time that they have. So, don't be so quick to give up on a goal. Be sure to evaluate your family's performance. If you are sure that everyone properly used the skill as intended, then consider moving on to different goals.

Enlist supporters, friends and partners in your goals; don't lone-wolf your goals. If you think you can accomplish your goal alone, you are sorely mistaken and can even end up struggling more to reach your goals. Most superheroes have side-kicks or civilians that they rely on for help and information. There's a reason for that. You need a community like extended family, a church, neighborhood association, or support group to support and help you. Connecting with community gives you feedback, accountability, and encouragement. Supporters can help you when things get hard, lift your spirits when you've had setbacks, and celebrate your victories with you after a win. Trust me, when you are making some hard changes, you want people in your court. Setting and accomplishing a goal is incredibly hard work and its life-changing. Don't do it alone.

At the risk of sounding repetitive, I'll state it again: change is hard. Because it's hard, it's important to give each other a lot of grace and understanding when trying new things. Allow some room for failure. In fact, I would suggest you reframe failure as a good thing. Failure allows learning to happen. Think of failure as information regarding what doesn't work — and you definitely want to know what doesn't work. Having identified what doesn't work, you'll discover what *does* work all the easier. Think of Thomas Edison's famous adage "I have not failed. I've just found **10,000** ways that won't work." You too will have your moments of discovering what doesn't work, but don't let it ruin your chances of success.

3 I also suggest you intentionally focus on progress and not perfection. It's easy to get stuck in a perfectionistic viewpoint when trying new things. Avoid this! Perfectionism kills motivation when trying new and difficult things. Instead, whenever you see progress in your family, congratulate yourself and praise others immediately. Families who overcome obstacles, accept that change is incremental. Always make sure to praise, acknowledge, and affirm progress, in whatever form, big or small. Be sure to make your praise substantive by praising someone's effort. Let them know what it is that you are praising.

The other benefit to praising progress, other than maintaining motivation, is that it affords opportunity for feedback. Whenever families are trying new things, feedback is crucial. Expect growing pains, which are not signs that change isn't happening or isn't possible, but rather signals that something is different When you praise, acknowledge, and affirm, it makes it safe to give feedback. If you don't praise, acknowledge, and affirm progress — but instead offer feedback devoid of support — your feedback comes off as a critique or attack. When someone feels critiqued or attacked, motivation is killed. This is a team effort. Keep your focus on building your team up instead of tearing it down.

| Family Story | The Christianson's were plagued with constant disappointment. The casual observer would think the Christianson family didn't have any problems — the perfect family. Nothing could have been further from the truth. Tom, the father, ran himself ragged trying to take care of everyone else, especially his youngest daughter, Lisa. For the most part, everyone appreciated Tom's efforts, but for Lisa who was 12 years old, she used the connection with her father and his desire to please, to wiggle out of normal expectations and boundaries. Her behavior was appalling. The more she complained, demanded and protested, the greater her control over her father with every whim and request. She often would aggressively berate, accuse, mock and belittle her father when Tom denied or was unable to give in to her wants. Over time, Lisa's behavior became too much for Tom and he'd explode. He'd get so angry and bitter he'd drink all night, terrorizing the house with angry rants. Per usual, he'd wake up the following morning late, profusely apologize, and without skipping a beat, go right back into his codependent behavior.

Seeking help the family began to work with a family therapist who gave them great suggestions, but did not provide structured goals and objectives. Their efforts never amounted to meaningful change and after a few months of participating in counseling, they were back to square one. Persistent, the family a different family therapist. However, this round of therapy was different. Much of the same ground was discussed and explored with the family, and the concept of crafting a concrete and measurable plan replete with specific goals and objectives was introduced. This enabled them to achieve sustained, meaningful change.

The Christianson's story is not everyone's. Not every family possesses the self-awareness that a problem exists. Not every family is willing to engage in therapy, twice. But the only thing that stands between them and an unsuccessful family is to learn from setbacks and a solid plan. It was the failure of the first round of therapy (the setback) that highlighted the family's need for a plan and, in turn, it was the plan that enabled the family to track success or check for needed adjustments in their behaviors.

Chapter 9

Paradoxical Nature of Success

To those of you who are experiencing success, who have implemented the ideas, skills, and strategies put forth in this book, be leery of success. I've worked with many families that, because of their success, think they can relax, think that they are out of the woods. But this can actually set you up for failure if you are like one of those families.

Why? It has to do with the paradoxical nature of success. Families make the mistake of thinking initial signs of success mean that the problem is over, that they no longer need to put forth the same amount of effort that got them the positive results. In other words, they shift into *cruise control* — and this is dangerous for three reasons.

1 What controlled your family up to the crisis and during the crisis were the family roles and toxic patterns of behavior. The desired goal now is the reverse: family roles that promote *healthy* and *positive patterns* of behavior. When a problem is not present, it doesn't mean you are excused from putting in the hard work. You are not excused from having to be consistent you definitely don't get a pass. The absence of a problem does not equal growth.

There's an idea in the field of psychology called *substitution*, which will help illustrate my point here. Substitution can easily be defined as the following: when changing a behavior, it is unhelpful simply to stop the behavior. Simply, if all you do is stop a behavior (not work on the processes and problems that perpetuate the behavior), you are likely to return to that behavior. Let's say I want to lose weight, and my biggest challenge to losing weight is eating ice cream. So, I cut ice cream out of my diet entirely, but I'm really struggling because I love ice cream. In my effort to keep my resolve strong, I tell myself, "Don't eat ice cream" over and over again. If I do this day in and day out, it will become the object of my attention and affection. Fixating on ice cream will eventually crumble my resolve and I will succumb to my love of ice cream once more; thus, preventing my weight loss from coming to fruition.

So what's the solution to this problem? What psychologists have found is that stopping an unwanted behavior is only the first half of the change equation. You have to stop the behavior and then substitute something else in its place. That means refocusing your attention on what you are going to *start* doing. Here is where your attention should lie, *on the behavior you are going to start.*

Let's return to my ice cream example. I want to lose weight, and ice cream is my biggest obstacle to that goal, so I cut ice cream out of my diet. (This is all purely theoretical since I do not plan on cutting out of my diet ice cream in any way, shape, or form.) Then, instead of fixating on what I'm not doing, I shift my focus to what I am doing or want to do. What is it that I want to do? I want to eat healthy. I want to increase the presence of delicious healthy food into my diet. This becomes my new "object" of attention and affection. Applying specific behaviors such as researching healthy recipes online and adjusting my shopping habits to buy healthier ingredients instead of unhealthy foods I usually gravitate towards. I might also engage my community by talking with friends and family members about healthy habits and how they too can make changes or just offer support. Lo and behold, my new health commitment sticks. I am able to go the distance with the changes I've made. Substitution does not guarantee that changes will stick, but it does increase the likelihood that they will.

2 Initial success is an indication that the changes you've made are working. You should be motivated to keep going by feeling a sense of accomplishment. The initial success provides the momentum to then address deeper changes that need to be made. Think of a ladder. Each rung you climb presents a new challenge. Some rungs will be easier than others, and some will feel incredibly difficult. For example, perhaps you and your family have trouble communicating because of deep hurt and betrayal. Through counseling or reading this book or the assistance of other sources of help, you've learned to communicate better. So far, so good. Now use those newfound skills and that momentum from positive change to address that deep hurt and betrayal. Get every ounce of utility out of your success.

Like I said before, the absence of a problem does not equal success. Progress is the effective application of a skill to a problem, in real time, that leads to positive results. Meaning that if you stop using the skill, you'll stop making progress. In a manner of speaking, family progress is like a muscle. To keep a muscle strong, you have to use it. When you stop using it, the skill will atrophy and begin creating hurt for the surrounding muscles. This is where self-discipline, or family discipline, becomes essential to maintaining family success. Be consistent and disciplined, even when you feel like you don't need to be.

3

Another danger that faces families who experience success is being unable to identify what works. I've worked with families that are satisfied after having a good week. For me, that's a golden opportunity to figure out what worked. To not investigate and identify what the family did differently is a tremendous loss. Instead of treating a good week like a happy accident, they can investigate and put to use what they identify — reduced stress, effective application of a skill, choosing not to act out a dysfunctional family role — with purpose. They can practice those things intentionally to get the same positive results. They can relish and celebrate the hard work put into the changes. It is essential to investigate and discover the reasons you are in a good place rather than just accepting that you are in a good place and carrying on ignorantly.

Ask yourself these questions to draw attention to what is working: *What did I do differently this week than before? Or, what changed around me? Why did it work?*

Family Story | The Felix family struggled bitterly with Greg, their teenage son. He had a history of drug use, involvement with gang-affiliated peers, selling drugs, and running away — very serious issues that caused the family great concern.

Greg's behavior outside the home affected family life inside the home. His parents were suspicious of him. They didn't trust him. Greg resented the fact that his parents didn't trust him. And all this tension, boiling under the surface, would bubble up and explode when it came to simple things like chores, staying at a friend's house over the weekend, use of the family car, and so forth.

Challenging the family with many of the skills outlined in this book, the family began to work towards a healthy relationship with each other. After some time and a great deal of hard work, the family started to see change. Things were going so well, they even had problem-free weeks. Tempted to congratulate myself and the family for their success, I instead switched my mindset to curiosity. I asked them several questions to get a sense of what was going on, what was different, what they were doing differently, what was different at work or at school or even with the weather. And what I learned from their answers shocked me.

Counseling was playing a helpful role, but as it turns out it wasn't the central cause for their growth. The transformation came from things they were learning on their own. For example, we had previously discussed (in session) the idea of considering the needs of your family member and how those needs may be different than your own. After listening to what I said in session, the mom remembered a book she read years before called *The Five Love Languages* by Gary Chapman.[11] She then reread the book and prompted her family to read it as well Taking the material from the book, they

---
[11] Chapman, Gary (2015). The Five Love Languages. Northfield Publishing.

then started treating each other with everyone's identified love language in mind (for those of you not familiar, these 5 languages are the way each of us give and receive love from others). The family managed to create change on their own and it led to their success.

There was still something about the family that puzzled me. When I had started counseling with them, Greg was very resistant to working on issues with family, especially with his mom. He and Mom were the ones who fought the most. So what prompted him to receive an idea from her about something that he was initially resistant to? When asked Greg expressed that he was open to the idea after his mom came to him. She approached him. For Greg, that meant a great deal. Because he felt like everyone in his family thought of him as "the problem," he turned to the gang who offered more of what felt like familial love and connection than his own biological family. As his mom approached him with the intent to make their relationship better, he realized that she cared.

As I validated the family's efforts and work in using the love languages as a resource, I identified for the family that it paled in comparison to what Greg had disclosed. Their insight and combined effort in trying something new and different was the reason they were experiencing success. When they as a family went out of their way to show how they care about each other, that is what made the difference. The family needed reassurance that, in the long run, demonstration of care and love will help them cultivate their relationship. This remains the key for them and for every other family out there. This process is like a spiral the more you follow it the more it draws inward – the more you follow and act on what works for your family, the more you draw closer to your family.

Success is clearly the point of all your hard work, but success ought to come with a warning sticker: "This product may be hazardous to the wellbeing of your family if you get complacent." I celebrate your success and urge you not to shift into cruise control because things are currently good. Keep working hard. Make these positive changes last for the life of your family.

Chapter 10

Maintaining Positive Change

Maintaining positive change takes work. Like a farmer, it takes more than planting seeds to produce a good crop. There are a number of tasks that follow planting which ensure a successful harvest. You have to tend, nurture, reassess, modify efforts, take a break, add new techniques, develop goals. This is hard work, but it pays off. If your family has followed the advice laid out in this book thus far, that means you have put a great deal of work into getting out of the crisis and creating change. Let's summarize your effort thus far:

- You've shifted your focus

- You no longer blame an individual or event for the crisis

- Everyone in the family has recognized the toxic pattern of behavior as the real problem

- Everyone has identified the dysfunctional family role they play that perpetuates the pattern

- Everyone has committed to change and is actively using skills to prevent or redirect the toxic pattern of behavior

- Some things worked and some things didn't as result of these new efforts in the family

- Everyone was brave enough to offer and receive heartfelt feedback on what could improve

- Everyone has made an effort to affirm and praise each other for the success in the family

- Everyone has worked hard to avoid success trap and has pushed through complacency

Look at all of your hard work! You have managed to get through some really tough and emotionally draining stuff and all of this has led to great success in the family (which everyone has once more made an effort to affirm and praise each other for). If this isn't success, I don't know what is. This is a tremendous achievement and ought to be celebrated. You ought to feel good. So what's left to do? Are there any more steps to consider? How do you, as a family, maintain long-term, sustainable growth? Here are four suggestions on how to make your growth sustainable.

1 Families need to always keep in mind what works. Even though the knowledge of what works is invaluable, families have a tendency to forget. There's no nefarious design behind this. Family life is busy. You're juggling a lot of balls at once. Because of this, it can be difficult to remember to practice the behaviors, skills, and mindsets that work. To overcome this problem, I often suggest that families create *reminders* of what works. Put up sticky notes around your house. Set a reminder notification on your smartphone. Create a song. Make a commemorative plaque as a family with the reminders of what works and display it prominently in your home. Or come up with something entirely different. The point is, whatever you choose to do and however you do it, you as a family need to regularly remind yourselves of what works.

Here are a few examples of reminders of what to do from clients I've worked with in the past.

- Writing on a whiteboard what does work.

- Putting inspiring quotes or mantras throughout the house.

- Touchstones- an object that helps everyone remember what they overcame. Could be a stone, photo, or sculpture.

2 It's only fitting that now I invite you to identify what doesn't work. This idea isn't suggested to create conflict or to rub your nose in past mistakes. Things may be on the up-and-up, but that doesn't mean there aren't lingering issues that need to be addressed. Addressing a problem doesn't spoil the positive momentum created by success. Just as you need to pursue what works, you also need to avoid what doesn't. Listing out what doesn't work as a family helps you do that. Being creative during this time also works well to help us remember what *not* to do. A couple simple examples for little kids might be "Hands are for helping, not hitting" or "Mouths are for munching macaroni and cheese, not biting your sister."

Here are a few examples of reminders of what not to do from clients I've worked with in the past.

- Be mindful of your family members areas of ongoing hurt and commit to being sensitive to them.

- Use a codename to alert each to the toxic pattern of behavior starting.

- Stay committed to feedback and repairing damage to family bonds.

3 My third suggestion is to create family rituals. Please don't be weirded out by the term *rituals*. I'm not suggesting you start performing animal sacrifices in your living room. By "rituals" I mean family norms that everyone takes part in and are repeated over time, like having a family meal together on a regular basis or having one evening per week dedicated to family time (i.e., pizza night on Sundays or game night on Fridays).

Here are a few examples of family rituals from clients I've worked with in the past.

- Cooking a meal together every week.

- Having a movie night.

- Playing games together.

- Reading books together.

4 Finally, I want you to come up with a plan for future family growth. In order to explain what I mean by this, I'll borrow a term from the business world. Entrepreneurs have used the term *vision-casting* to capture the idea of looking into the future and imagining what you want and what you need to do in order to get what you want. I want you to do some vision-casting for your own family. Imagine what your family could be. Think of the next step for your family. How could things be even better than they are right now? Better still, this process can be a beautiful way of working together as a family and to continue building connection. Capitalize on that!

Here are a few examples of vision-casting from clients I've worked with in the past.

- A written plan outlining what does work, what doesn't work, and the family's goal to continue their growth prominently displayed on the fridge.

- Accountability- Each member of the family commits to each other that they will continue making steps towards positive growth.

- Accountability 2.0- The family, as a whole, commits to another family, or church or community of some kind, to continue making growth together.

- Schedule a future date everyone will get together, whether things are good or bad, to discuss and evaluate how things are going.

Chapter 11

When You Need Outside Help

There is something to be said about admitting when you aren't able to resolve a struggle on your own. It can be a difficult and vulnerable process, but it may be necessary to bring in outside help, an objective third-party who can give you observations and feedback.

Ideally, as you reach out for help, you would know to search for a trained professional such as a licensed marriage and family therapist or an experienced licensed mental health counselor (also known as a licensed professional counselor depending on the state) with appropriate education in family therapy. However, I have discovered that families are often confused regarding the field of counseling and the roles counselors play. This fact gets further complicated when families are in crisis and need help immediately because there may not be the time to dedicate significant thought into the different types of counselors and models of therapy. Consider this chapter as a short primer on the field.

What Are the Different Types of Mental Health Professionals?

Not every mental health professional is the same. Mental health professionals vary in education, degrees, training, and specialization. Therefore, it is incumbent on you and your family to be informed as to which mental health professional may be the best match for your needs. Take a look at the list below in order to know and identify the counselor which may be right for you and your family.

Mental Health Counselor: Mental health counselor is titled differently depending on the state. In some states, the regulating board or department titles this license as Licensed Mental Health Counselor (LMHC). In other states, it is Licensed Professional Counselor (LPC); the two licenses are essentially the same. Both demand Master's degree level education, internships, and other training requirements to hold this type of credential. Licensed master's level counselors provide diagnoses and treat a wide range of mental illnesses. These counselors typically treat individuals, but many specialize. Some of those specialties include anxiety, depression, mood disorders, PTSD/trauma, play therapy, gender identity, and even in couples or family therapy. If you are seeking services from an LMHC or LPC, it's always best practice to ensure they have completed the appropriate training to work with couples and families often this looks like additional Master's level courses or extended seminars. Counselors also specialize in treating a multitude of disorders. It's also important to note that some disorders such as Autism Spectrum Disorders may be required in some states to be assessed by Doctorate level clinicians (see psychologists and psychiatrists below).

Relationship Counselor: Licensed Marriage and Family Therapists are providers who specialized in treating families and couples. While they often have the same education base as Mental Health Clinicians, LMFT's often choose to complete additional training during their Master's degree – qualifying them for the more detailed license title. The license requires a Master's, PhD (Doctor of Philosophy in Psychology) or PsyD (Doctor of Psychology). Despite the seemingly specific education, LMFT's can work with individuals and can have additional areas of expertise much like LPCs or LMHCs.

Addiction Counselor: Addiction counselor – a title that varies from state to state. In some states, the title is Chemical Dependency Counselor, Substance Abuse Counselor, Alcohol and Drug Counselor, Addiction Counselor. Regardless of title, these clinicians are trained in diagnosing and treating substance abuse and sometimes comorbid disorders (two or more disorders in the same client such as Alcohol Use Disorder and Depression or Cannabis Use Disorder and General Anxiety Disorder). Levels of education range from Associate's and Bachelor's degrees up to Master's and PhD's. In some states, these providers are only able to treat addiction disorders if they have an Associate's or Bachelor's degree. Feel free to investigate a potential counselor's credentials and even ask them what disorders they are able to treat. Information seeking is always to great way to find a great provider.

Social Worker: A person can get a Bachelor's, Master's, or PhD degree in Social Work. The field of Social Work aims to help individuals, couples, and families that are in need. Their goal for their clients is to access the right resources given the situation their clients are experiencing. Although not trained primarily in counseling, some social workers also provide counseling. Similarly, to LMFTs, it is always in your best interest to touch base with any social workers you are interested in working with to find out if they have had what we call clinical training. This ensures that the provider you choose has expertise and training in psychotherapy.

Psychiatrist: Psychiatrists carry the MD or Medical Doctor designation. This means that they attended medical school followed by their completion of a psychiatric residency (a 3 to 4-year training program following the completion of medical school). Not only do they attempt to resolve medical issues from which psychiatric symptoms are occurring, they also treat mental illness through psychotropic medications. While most know psychiatrists as prescribers only, some do focus on and offer psychotherapy in addition to prescribing.

Psychologist: Psychologists are doctoral level clinicians in the field of psychology. The letters that follow their name are noted as PhD or PsyD. Theses practitioners who have been trained to do research, teach, provide counseling, and psychological assessments. A psychologist can provide and evaluate numerous psychological batteries aka tests that assess personality, psychological disorders, and even neurological issues. Colloquially, these evaluations are known as Psych Evals. It is important to remember that not all PhDs are psychologists. PhD's are awarded in *many* doctoral degrees from the arts to the sciences and to education and business. That being said, all PsyD's are psychologists and specialize in psychotherapy and clinical work. Earning a Doctor of Philosophy in Psychology doesn't always mean that individuals provide therapy. Some teach and some do research. When in doubt, seeking information is always a great answer.

Psychiatric Nurse Practitioner: Qualifications for psychiatric Nurse Practitioners, require a minimum of a Master's degree, but earn a PhD or a Doctor of Nursing Practice in Psychiatry. A Psychiatric Nurse Practitioner can diagnose, prescribe and therapeutically treat clients. Their role in the clinical world is to help individuals access psychiatric medications to help manage symptoms. They typically don't specialize in psychotherapy and instead refer to the previously listed providers for that type of service.

Wrap-Around Service: A wrap-around service is a team of people, usually a mix of professionals like counselors, care coordinators, social workers, peer support, and family and youth advocates who are based out of local mental health agencies. They provide intensive services for families who qualify for services. The team will move quickly to understand the various factors contributing to the family issues and address them through an over-arching plan that include the voices and collective of the team, including that of the family.

Given the particulars of a family crisis, a family may need to utilize the services or a number of mental health professionals. For example, in order to identify a mental illness, a family may need to engage the services of a psychologist to conduct a full psychological evaluation to accurately diagnose. Based on diagnosis or diagnoses given, a course of psychological treatment may be recommended, including the services of a psychiatrist or psychiatric nurse practitioner for medication, a medical doctor to address a physical issue, a social worker to help a family access community services, or a mental health counselor to provide counseling. There's not correct order of operations, but successful treatment usually involves a number of mental health professionals coordinating together.

What Are Common Issues that Affect Families?

Just as different types of provider play different roles, different types of mental health issues may be contributing to the crisis your family find itself in. Therefore, these mental health issues need to be identified and treated with the appropriate mental health services for your family to get all the help it can get. For example, your family may be limited in their ability to get out of the crisis due to a family members unaddressed depression.[12] Accurately identifying and understanding the nature of a family member's issue will allow the family to be more effective in their support and better equipped at finding appropriate treatment. Yet the issue is not necessarily localized to an individual. It could be an issue that affects several or all family members. The following is a list of problem areas that cause families to seek out counseling.

Mental Illness: *Mental illness* refers to a wide range of mental health disorders and issues that affect your mood, how you feel, and how you think. A few examples of mental health disorders include Major Depressive Disorder (depression), Anxiety Disorders, Personality Disorders, Eating Disorders, and Addiction Disorders. Counselors help families develop coping strategies to manage and overcome these and other mental health disorders. Unaddressed mental health issues can cause relational damage in families and a search on the internet won't suffice.

---

[12] To learn more about supporting a family member struggling with depression see *Appendix B* for more information.

Proper training to detect and assess for a mental health diagnosis takes years and a 2 hours binge of WebMD isn't the same. Sometimes there are things that only those who are trained know and understand about diagnoses that get missed by a basic web search. As an example, many clients will come in stating depression as their main source of distress when in reality they are discussing traits of an anxiety disorder. Therefore, it is critical to find and work with a competent mental health professional who can provide such a service.

For example, depression can greatly impact an individual and how they relate to their family members. It can feel like the person you once knew is gone and has been replaced by a depressed version. It can be hard to support to them and know how to connect.[13] This holds true for a number of mental health issues. Parents aren't at their best when they have chronic pain and anxiety. A sibling isn't as playful when their OCD doesn't allow them to touch certain toys. The bond with grandparents can take a big hit when dementia makes it hard to remember basic facts of their own history and relationship with you. A proper diagnosis along with proper treatment make not immediately solve the problem, which may endure for a long period of time, but having a name for the problem helps families understand and support more effectively.

Addiction: Addiction is a person's inability to control their use of a substance or behavior due to a number of causes. An individual's addiction may

---

[13] Ibid.

be kept secret from their family, may be enabled by their family, or may create friction and conflict in their family. Addiction has a serious impact on family relationships and that impact will need to be addressed in individual and family counseling.

Traumatic Brain Injuries: Injuries to the brain can cause a number of issues to individuals such as mood swings, memory impairment, personality changes, and sleep issues among other symptoms. It can also affect an individual's relationships and how they relate to their family members. I've worked with a number of families where a child has had sports related injury causing a traumatic brain injury. Parents have reported to me that their child seems to be a different person after the injury or series of injuries and they no longer know how to relate to their "new kid."

Job Loss: Losing a job can affect an individual and how they relate to their family. The individual may feel a loss of identity, guilt for not bringing in an income, and grave uncertainty about their vocational future. This can put an emotional wedge between them and the other family members, not to mention the increased stress due the loss of income that everyone is likely feeling. Stress and uncertainty can either bond a family together or tear them apart. Or, exacerbate existing, yet unobvious mental health problems.

Blended Family Dynamic: As if family life isn't hard enough, making a blended family work may seem impossible. There are all sorts of issues that arise from blending families together, which can either exacerbate a crisis or create one.[14]

Trauma: Trauma results from a person experiencing a terrible situation or viewing another person endure a terrible situation. This experience causes emotional pain and harm that continues into the future potentially impacting family relationships negatively.

When to Seek Out Counseling?

Due to a number of factors, it can be hard to know when its time to acknowledge your family's need for counseling. One of the reasons it can be hard is because every family is different, every individual is different, and there aren't black and white rules for when to seek out counseling. Generally, when problems impair a family's ability to function such as effectively communicate, problem solve, work through conflict, demonstrate respect, and connect in a positive way, you may consider accessing counseling services. Problems may also occur from going through difficult circumstances like divorce, custody issues, death, job loss, problems in school, infidelity and financial issues, which may also require counseling services. The mistake families often make is to ignore the problem, to wait and hope it goes away, or to make an attempt to fix the problem, and if it doesn't immediately lead to a successful resolution, then assume that any every attempt to work through the problem won't work.

---

[14] To learn more about the blended family dynamic, see *Appendix D* for more information.

So, families allow issues to develop and grow, until they become very serious issues that cause a great deal of harm. It is better to prevent a problem before it has time to mature into an issue that is unwieldy. Therefore, I recommend a proactive approach and to seek out a counselor early in the genesis of a family crisis.

How to Pick a Good Counselor?

If you do choose to seek out a counselor, you'll want to be selective in who you work with. Fit is everything. Let me say that again, *fit is everything*. Finding the right counselor for your family can be a difficult task. There are so many things to consider and evaluate when looking for a counselor that it is easy to get overwhelmed. Being overwhelmed by the process will likely lead you either to give up and not get the counseling you need or settle for a counselor who isn't qualified or isn't the right fit for your family. To overcome this challenge, there are five things to look for that will help you find a qualified, professional, and effective counselor.

Education: Having the proper education does not guarantee your counselor is a good one, but education does sift the wheat from the chaff. Highly qualified counselors often have a bachelor's degree in Psychology, Human Development, Sociology, Social Work, or a related field, *and* a master's degree in Social Work, Psychology, Mental Health Counseling, or Chemical Dependency. It's important to inquire as to a potential candidate's credentials and verify their license. States usually have online directories that allow you to access information regarding the credentials of the potential counselors. Licenses ensure that a counselor has been vetted and will be held accountable to the legal and ethical standards set by the state.

Empathy: It's important to find a counselor who puts in the effort to create a safe and positive relationship with you. Look for someone who authentically connects with you, who makes the effort to understand where you're coming from, what you think, and how you feel about things. That isn't to say a good counselor always agrees with you or endorses your perspective or decisions. A good counselor will challenge you and sometimes give you difficult feedback, but it should come from a place of empathy and genuine care.

Expertise: Look for a counselor who has expertise with the problem you are dealing with. This raises the question, what is expertise? When counselors first enter the mental health field they are like general practitioners — they have general knowledge of mental health disorders and how to treat them. But only after years of study, counseling, and training do counselors establish themselves as experts on a particular psychological or relational issue. Let's take a look at an example. You are dealing with a parenting issue, and you should contact a parenting expert (also known as a Filial Therapist). If you have an addiction issue, you'll want to see a Chemical Dependency Counselor. If you have an eating disorder, you'll want to see a counselor who specializes in treatments for those diagnoses. Having an expert properly diagnose what a family member is struggling with can immensely benefit your family. Once you have identified the disorder, family members can more effectively support each other from a position of knowledge and understanding. For example, if a family member is diagnosed with major depressive disorder, it will be incumbent on every family member to learn and gain an understanding of the disorder. Otherwise, their efforts to support may be ill-informed and ineffective, or, even worse, their expectations for their family member may be inappropriate and create harm.[15]

Evidence-Based Therapy: You will want to see a counselor who has been trained in and practices an evidenced-based model of psychotherapy.[16] This means that the techniques, models, and interventions have been researched and proven to be effective. There are many counselors who practice their own version of psychotherapy, which may or may not be effective. In other words, when you work with incompetent counselors, you are taking a gamble. However, when you see a counselor who practices an evidence-based therapy, who has experience and training, you increase the chances that counseling will be effective. Additionally, most evidence-based therapy models require additional

---

[15] To learn more about how you can support a family member with a common mental health disorder like major depressive disorder, see *Appendix B*.

[16] An evidence-based model of psychotherapy is category assigned to models of therapy that have been rigorously tested and scrutinized by researchers in order to assess whether they are effective or not when it comes to helping clients.

training, supervision, and follow-up trainings. This is a good thing because it ensures your counselor is competently trained, is held accountable for the quality of their treatment, and has support from other mental health professionals.

Empowerment: Most importantly, you want to see a counselor who is an expert but not a know-it-all. Specifically, experts have knowledge of a specific problem, but just because they are well versed in psychology doesn't mean they know everything about you. A good counselor will learn your story and empower you to make the changes you need based on your goals. A good counselor will follow what works for you while lending their guidance and feedback when needed.

It is totally appropriate for you to ask questions of your counselor, verify their licensing and credentials, and look them up before you make your initial contact. It is perfectly appropriate for you to advocate for your family and for what you want before and after the counseling relationship is established. If your counselor is not willing to provide what you are looking for or if they aren't comfortable or properly trained, then ask for a referral. Be okay in also asking for a referral in instances where you feel the counselor you work with is not a good fit. You are not meant to jive with everyone and counselors are never offended if client's feel the fit is off. This process is about you and your family. A good counselor will help you find what you are looking for, even if that means you seeing someone else. But make sure you are changing counselors not because they properly challenged you and it made you uncomfortable, but because they don't offer what you need. Do not disguise your avoidance of discomfort with a disingenuous complaint with your counselor.

Hopefully, the Five *E*s will help guide you in your search for a good therapist. There is no guarantee you'll find the perfect therapist, but any good counselor worth their salt will have the Five *E*s.

What is the Process of Counseling?

Counseling at a basic level is a *relationship*. A family works with a counselor to get help with a problem, but the relationship you have with your counselor is unlike most professional relationships. For example, with a doctor, you go in for an appointment when there is a problem, and they give you a treatment that fixes the problem. A mechanic is another great example. You drop your car off, and in few hours, you pick up a fixed car. While you might trust your doctor or your mechanic's expertise, they generally are working on physical solutions, not emotional ones. Your mechanic might not care about the conflict with your children or spouse. Yet, with a counselor, a trusting relationship is absolutely necessary. They *do* care about your emotions and family patterns are integral to the solutions.

Families seeking counseling might experience thoughts of *Why is this person trying to get to know me? What does number of kids in my family matter? Why does the counselor want to know about our family history, substance use, relational patterns, medical history, and social life?* Counselors want to know those details because they want and sometimes need to get to know your family. Yes, the specific concern for which you are coming to counseling is a priority to them, but it's not the chief priority. What matters to a counselor most is who you are as a family, how your family thinks and feels. Having gained this understanding, then, and only then, will your family and your counselor start to address the problem. The context of your family patterns serves as the springboard for addressing what's going on.

Additionally, counselors want to get to know your family because that helps *contextualize* the problem. The *why, how, when, what,* and *who* is very important for understanding what's going on. Counseling is not a simple as "If *x*, then *y*." Emotions are confusing. People are messy. Relationships are complicated. Family history can be difficult to sort through. Counselors are task with becoming very well acquainted with your family quickly and chunks of time that are shorter than an episode of Game of Thrones. Talk about pressure. Therefore, you need to give your counselor time. Counseling is not about getting quick, simplistic answers.

To put it another way, counselors aren't mechanics. You can't simply come into the counseling office to fix or replace one part of your life like you can with your car. A parent's dysfunctional communication pattern with their teenager isn't like a misfiring spark plug. Overcoming an addiction isn't like fixing a broken catalytic converter. Engaging in counseling is a process of identifying problem behaviors and patterns, learning new habits, practicing by trial and error, adjusting to a new "normal," being discouraged after a setback, finding support, gaining some success, and maintaining new, healthy behaviors. In other words, counseling is really hard work and let's face it, counselors can only work as hard as you are working. It isn't easy to change and your counselor can't change for you. Change requires that you emotionally, relationally, and spiritually engage in your own pain and discomfort.

Furthermore, everyone is limited by their own experiences, knowledge, maturity level, and perspective. It is very difficult to objectively evaluate your own behavior, thinking, and relationships. Therefore, it is helpful and sometimes necessary to get an outside perspective. You want a knowledgeable, impartial, empathic perspective and counselors are trained to provide just that. Counselors know the right questions to ask. They are adept at listening to understand, not to judge or condemn. They can tease out hidden assumptions, provide insightful feedback, and offer creative and helpful suggestions. They know when to take the wheel and when to sit back and let you drive.

People chronically avoid facing pain and discomfort. It is the human condition to want to maximize pleasure and reduce discomfort. This is a natural response to most issues in life, but what is natural isn't always beneficial. Why? When you avoid pain, discomfort, conflict, and problems, they don't magically go away. In fact, they tend to get worse (think dust bunnies under your couch – they hide everywhere and multiply). It may seem counterintuitive, but pressing into the pain, understanding your discomfort, and working through problems with the help of a counselor enables growth, change, and healing. That's the "big picture" reasoning for the need of counseling and why it can be helpful.

What Are the Goals of Family Therapy?

You and your family can either partner with the counselor and squeeze every ounce of usefulness out of counseling, or you can resist the process and push your family deeper down a hole. The choice is yours. I'd suggest the collaborate/partnering approach. By focusing and engaging with the goals listed below, you will be partnering and therefore empowering the counseling process.

Change the Status Quo: Marriage and Family Therapy can feel like a scary, threatening, nerve-racking process. Why? Family Therapy threatens the status quo, which families guard fiercely because the status quo feels safe and familiar, even if its unhealthy. If the status quo is exposed to be unhealthy, then change is required, and change, well, frankly is uncomfortable. Change requires hard work and taking responsibility for bad behavior. It also requires engaging with hurt and pain. A family may want to avoid that discomfort, and if allowed, they also avoid the opportunity for change and growth. Yet, when your family can embrace and work through hurt, the door is open to healing and growth. An effective LMFT will walk your family through this process.

Create a Relational Focus: It is very easy for families to blame one person or one event for all their problems. That said, this hyper-focus is a serious mistake if families truly want to see change and progress. It is far better when families look at what isn't working with a *relational focus*. This may be hard to achieve on your own, therefore, the help of a LMFT can help you think in a new way. They will help your family adopt a relational focus, which is seeing how each member's behavior contributes to a problem. This is not done for the purpose of assigning blame, but for taking responsibility. When family members take responsibility for their personal contribution to the problem, it creates an environment where change is safe to do. Otherwise, it may feel too threatening to be vulnerable and try something new.

Identify and Meet Needs: Not everyone is the same. Not everyone has the same needs. This may seem like an obvious truth, but all too often family members act in opposition to this idea. They believe that the other person has the same needs as them. So, when they try to fulfill the other person's needs, they do so in a way that makes sense to *themselves* and not *others*. Rather they believe that the family should know what their needs are and so fulfill them without explicitly stating their needs. Either way, this approach doesn't work. An LMFT will be able to expertly observe and point out the different needs of each of the members and teach the family to honor each other's needs. You must be open to learning about the needs of your family members — which may be different than your own — and commit to meeting those needs.

Reciprocate: The exciting thing about discovering what your family member's needs are — versus falsely assuming what their needs are — is that when you meet those needs, the other person is more likely to *reciprocate*. Meaning, when they feel fulfilled, they will be motivated to make sure you feel fulfilled. This is a positive feedback loop that builds strength the longer it goes. The more you feel loved by the other, the more likely you are to return that love to them.

Learn New Skills: Successful families concluding treatment walk away from the experience with a new set of skills that empower them to break toxic patterns of behavior and create new, healthy patterns of behavior. Therefore, be open to learning new skills. For some families, they believe they've tried everything and nothing will work. That's often not the case. There may be many strategies and skills that families are not aware of that an LMFT can teach. Alternatively, families may have tried new skills, but quickly bailed on them when things were challenging. Again, an LMFT will not only teach skills, but coach families on how to consistently use them in an effective manner.

What Supplemental Counseling Services Exist?

In addition to family therapy, there are other types of counseling and mental health services which can supplement and support family therapy.

Filial Therapy: Parenting is hard — there are no two ways about it. The demands on modern parents are overwhelming. Balancing work, relationships, social life, and schedules can wear a person out. Thus, when issues crop up with your kids, life can come to a screeching halt. That's why it is important to seek help and insight from parenting experts who can point out problem patterns, effective strategies of communication and relationship skill building, and ideas on how to build a better relationship with your kids.

Career Counseling: Mental illness extends further than the counseling office. Mental illness can impact your career, in terms of what career you pursue, how you perform at work, and even how much fulfillment you experience. Career counselors are trained in ways that can help you find the career that best fits your passions and strengths or they can help you discover better coping strategies to deal with job-related stress, office conflict, and the work–life balance.

Psychiatric Care: Psychiatric care can involve a psychiatric evaluation where a diagnosis is made and medication is prescribed by a psychiatrist or psychiatric nurse practitioner. And there is usually follow up appointments to manage medication side effects and effectiveness. Psychiatric care can take place in an outpatient setting where a psychiatrist sees patients and provides diagnostic and prescription writing services. Psychiatric care can also take place in an inpatient setting where a team of medical and psychological services are provided in a safe and secure setting like a psych ward in a hospital, or at a behavioral health inpatient facility.

Psychological Evaluation: You may be dealing with a mental health condition that reaches beyond the scope of general mental health disorders. Conditions such as having an impaired memory, an inability to recognize faces, a traumatic brain injury, or other unique neurobiological problems that cannot be assessed by medical doctors or general mental health counselors. If this is the case, you may need to see a psychologist who specializes in evaluating and treating rare and unique psychological issues.

Addiction Treatment: Those successful in recovery typically engage in the services of a Chemical Dependency Counselor, Family Therapist, Licensed Mental Health Counselor or Licensed Professional Counselor, Social Worker, or Psychiatrist in a group therapy setting, in individual counseling in outpatient counseling, or check themselves into an inpatient treatment facility. Addiction treatment usually involves working with the family system since the family can play a role in enabling the addict and can be redirected to play a powerful role in supporting the addict's recovery.

Hopefully, this chapter has made you aware of what counseling is, how it works, and why your family may need it. If you feel like your family needs counseling, please *do not* put it off for too long. Families have a tendency to avoid problems, and that tends to make problems worse. If others close to you whom you trust, suggest counseling, listen to them. Choosing to pursue counseling can be one of the hardest and best decisions you can make for your family. The benefits will help your family for the rest of your life.

Epilogue

It is my hope that this book has been helpful to you. I have been greatly affected by the families I've worked with and I've seen people do extraordinary things with a sincere desire to get their families back on track. There is nothing more important than family and the relationships shared with them. I've also seen people extraordinarily obstinate, resisting the changes they so clearly need to make. They want things to be different, but they don't want to make any personal changes. It makes sense; change is uncomfortable. Discomfort forces you to take responsibility for your actions. Discomfort forces you to create a new normal. Discomfort forces you to break old habits and make new ones. It's tough work, and I am very empathetic to families that struggle. Take heart because the struggle leads somewhere good. Discomfort is the engine for positive change. So welcome discomfort into your life. Stop fighting it and use it to bring about the changes your family so desperately needs.

Appendix A

Domestic Violence and Abuse

Much of what has been said in this book applies, in general, to most families and most issues. In family issues and crises, there is a proper presumption of shared responsibility both in acknowledging the struggle each person has and creating change. Working through the problem as a family is the standard because generally, it took the whole family's effort to create the problem. However, in cases of domestic violence and abuse (DVA), the issue or crisis was not created by the group and there is no excuse for domestic violence and abuse. Victims of DVA are not to blame for their victimization. *They did not do anything to create or perpetuate the cycle of abuse.* In cases of domestic violence and abuse, the responsibility rests with one or two individuals, the abuser(s).

Before proceeding, it would be prudent to first define DVA. DVA is "any incident or pattern of incidents of controlling behavior, coercive behavior or threatening behavior, violence or abuse between those aged 16 or over who are family members or who are, or have been, intimate partners. This includes psychological, physical, sexual, financial and emotional abuse. It also includes 'honor'-based violence and forced marriage."[17] DVA is not reserved for only certain people. It can happen to any person or family regardless of socioeconomic status, race, religion, or sex. Men and women can be both abusers and victims of abuse. In a significant amount of relationships, one partner is the aggressor, but there are also occasions where both partners are abusive and violent towards each other. This situation has been termed as bi-directional intimate partner violence, or inter-partner violence.

Here's a breakdown of some alarming numbers about DVA:

- More than one in three women and more than one in four men in the United States have experienced rape, physical violence, and/or stalking by an intimate partner in their lifetime.

---

[17] Domestic violence and abuse - NICE quality standard [QS116]. Available from: https://www.researchgate.net/publication/307122415_Domestic_violence_and_abuse_-_NICE_quality_standard_QS116 [accessed Mar 03 2018].

- **74** percent of all murder-suicides involved an intimate partner (spouse, common-law spouse, ex-spouse or boyfriend/girlfriend). Of these, **96** percent were women killed by their intimate partners.

- One in five female high school students report being physically and/or sexually abused by a dating partner.

- Interpersonal violence is the leading cause of female homicides and injury-related deaths during pregnancy.

- The percentage of women who consider their mental health to be poor is almost three times higher among women with a history of violence than among those without.

- Women with disabilities have a **40** percent greater risk of intimate partner violence, especially severe violence, than women without disabilities.[18]

DVA is a very serious problem afflicting many families in the United States. Although you may feel helpless and powerless in your current situation, there are actions you can take to help you and your family if you are currently experiencing DVA.

---

[18] American Psychological Association. www.apa.org/topics/violence/partner.aspx?item=1. Retrieval Date: September 15th, 2017.

1 Find a caring and supportive network of friends and family who will listen to your story and be willing to help. Being in a DVA situation can feel isolating and lonely. The more isolated you are, the more susceptible you will be to psychological control and the weaker your position will be. You must be willing to reach out to others and share your story. You must also do this selectively. Sometimes family members and friends, when hearing your story, may take sides and may take the side of your abuser. Do not take this as an indication that you shouldn't reach out and share your story. You should, but wisely with people you can trust.

2 Don't be afraid to call the police. Getting the police involved may seem scary, it may seem like it will invite retribution from your abuser. But, having worked with many victims of DVA, they often express their regret for not calling the police when they should have. You will never feel safe or comfortable when calling the police; however, calling is the right choice. At the very least, it will produce to police report and a documented history of your abuser's actions. With police and other first responders becoming increasingly aware of DVA, more and more police departments are creating and launching domestic violence units whose sole purpose is to help victims access resources and even prosecute their partners if willing. They are there to help you. Take them up on it if you need to.

There are other legal avenues you can pursue like getting a restraining or no-contact order. Again, this provides you with legal protections against your abuser and can help you feel more secure. It also allows for you to begin taking back the power that is generally lost in an abusive relationship

3 Seek the help of a professional who has experience working with victims of DVA. There are many actions you can take to improve your situation and the situation for your family, but that will require you to work through your trauma and how your abuser has created psychological control. You will have to break free from that control in order to see options available and pursue them. This means that *family therapy is not an option.* Until safety can be established, stepping into the vulnerable setting of counseling puts victims at further risk for harm.

4 Be prepared with a safety/exit plan for you and your kids. This is certainly not the most comfortable thing to think about, but not thinking about it and being unprepared is not a great alternative. You have to think through likely worst-case scenario and imagine how you can keep yourself and your kids safe. Here are some helpful things to think through when making your safety/exit plan:

- Identify your partner's use and level of force so that you can tell when you and your children are in danger before it occurs.

- Identify safe areas of the house where there are no weapons (e.g., not the kitchen) and there are ways to escape. If arguments begin, try to move to one of those areas.

- If violence occurs, make yourself a small target — dive into a corner and curl up into a ball, with your face protected and arms around each side of your head, fingers entwined.

- If possible, have a phone handy at all times and know what numbers to call for help.

- Don't be afraid to call the police.

- Let trusted friends and neighbors know of your situation and develop a plan and visual signal for when you need help.

- Pack a bag and include money, an extra set of keys, copies of important documents (social security cards, birth certificates, car titles, driver's license, etc, extra clothes and medicines. Leave it in a safe place or with someone you trust.

- Teach your children how to get help. Instruct them not to get involved in the violence between you and your partner. Plan a code word to signal to them that they should get help or leave the house.

- Practice how to get out safely. Practice with your children.

- Call a domestic violence hotline periodically to assess your options and get support and understanding.[19]

---

[19] Ibid.

5 Reject the abuser's lies. A victim of DVA often believes they are the cause of their mistreatment or even that they deserve it. Abuse starves the victims from authentic love and connection and substitutes power and control as love. This dynamic usually results in the victim clinging to the only form of "love" they are receiving despite how dangerous or unhealthy the behaviors. They are also taught to think they are weak, powerless, and unintelligent and that they shouldn't bother family and friends with their problems. These beliefs are based on a lie created by the abuser to exert their control and power. An abused partner is controlled to the degree that he or she buys their abuser's lies.

If you are a victim of abuse, it is critical for you to understand that, in order to take back your life, you have to take responsibility for your part in believing the abuser's lies. Your abuser needs you to believe they are in control. Your abuser has crossed the line so many times you've lost count and have fallen into the trap of believing you are creating your own destruction. They've lied, cheated, hit, cursed, and intimidated. You know deep down that you should have left a hundred times by now, but you didn't. You didn't because you rationalized, minimized, and falsely believed you were powerless. When you take responsibility for your part, you take back control.

6 Be aware and informed of resources that can assist you. You are not alone. There are people and resources that can offer support, advice, suggestions, and help. You can access these resources unbeknownst to your abuser. These resources are within your reach if you have access to a phone or the internet. Here are some key resources to be aware of:

- <u>ADWAS: Abused Deaf Women's Advocacy Services</u> Provides comprehensive services to deaf and deaf-blind victims/survivors of sexual assault, domestic violence and stalking.

- <u>The APA's Psychologist Locator</u> Makes it easy for you to find practicing psychologists in your local area.

- <u>National Coalition Against Domestic Violence</u> Works to educate the public on how to recognize domestic violence and what to do about it; teen dating violence; the impact of family violence on children; and domestic violence against individuals with disabilities, older adults, and other marginalized populations.

- <u>VAWnet: The National Online Resources Center on Violence Against Women</u> Provides a comprehensive and easily accessible collection of full-text, searchable electronic materials and resources on domestic violence, sexual violence, and related issues.

- <u>Women of Color Network (WOCN)</u> Promotes and supports the leadership of women of color advocates.[20]

- The National Domestic Violence Hotline

- Call The National Domestic Violence Hotline at $1-800-799-7233$ or TTY $1-800-787-3224$. Their website address is: http://www.thehotline.org/.

---

[20] Ibid.

Appendix B

How to Support a Depressed Family Member

Depression is a widely misunderstood mental health disorder. Depression affects people's careers, sexuality, and physical and emotional health. One effect is often ignored because it lives on the periphery of our attention: family, friends, spouses, children, and significant others are also greatly affected by their loved one's depression. They too carry the burden of depression. Often, mental health treatment focuses only on the individual suffering from depression, but what about those who care for them? What are family members and significant others supposed to do when their loved one is in emotional pain? How can they help? How can they care for themselves when caring for their loved one? These important questions are rarely discussed. Below you will find ten guidelines to take when your loved one is depressed.

1 Realize that depression doesn't define your loved one. Depression can seem to change a person's personality; however, the change isn't permanent. Think of depression like turning the volume dial down on a speaker: it's still playing the same music, but at diminished level. Your family member is still the same person, they are behaving differently because of the depression. However, people recover from depression every day and regain their energy, their motivation, and most importantly, their personality. That person you once knew is still there.

2 Remember to take care of yourself. Caretaking and/or living with someone who is suffering from depression can be emotionally taxing. It is not selfish for you to take care of yourself and you also don't have to succumb to depression yourself. There is an appropriate level of emotional distance that is healthy both for your own wellbeing and for your loved one as well. Too much involvement in their mental illness can be a bad thing and creates more distress on the relationship. When you take care of yourself, you are also showing your loved one how to take care of themselves.

3 Have patience. Depending on what type of depression your loved one has, recovery can take a great deal of time. Know that there is a lot of trial and error involved in the recovery process. The reason is that depression compromises a person's motivation for healing. In many other types of mental illness, despite the gravity of the psychological issue, their motivation for healing and change can be strong. With depression, that motivation is greatly diminished. Without motivation for change, depression takes a long time to heal Have patience with your loved one and have patience through the process of healing. If they are taking medication, going to counseling, or attending a support group, give time for these treatments to work.

4 Maintain a predictable and regular schedule. Depression has a way of stalling life. It is like chewing molasses. Life becomes slow and arduous. This affects your loved one and it affects you as well. It's important to acknowledge that. Yet it doesn't have to overwhelm your life. You can still have dreams, goals, and ambitions while taking time to be there for your loved one. In fact, when your life is built on a foundation of structure, routine, and predictability, you create a stable environment. Stability is something your loved one needs when they feel like they are emotionally spiraling down.

5

Look for vicarious symptoms. Be watchful of your assumption of depressive symptoms demonstrated by your loved one., Have you noticed, in yourself, any of the following?[21]

- Feelings of sadness, tearfulness, emptiness or hopelessness

- Angry outbursts, irritability or frustration, even over small matters

- Loss of interest or pleasure in most or all normal activities, such as sex, hobbies or sports

- Sleep disturbances, including insomnia or sleeping too much

- Tiredness and lack of energy, so even small tasks take extra effort

- Reduced appetite and weight loss or increased cravings for food and weight gain

- Anxiety, agitation or restlessness

- Slowed thinking, speaking or body movements

- Feelings of worthlessness or guilt, fixating on past failures or blaming yourself for things that aren't your responsibility

- Trouble thinking, concentrating, making decisions and remembering things

- Frequent or recurrent thoughts of death, suicidal thoughts, suicide attempts or suicide

- Unexplained physical problems, such as back pain or headaches

---

[21] http://www.mayoclinic.org/diseases-conditions/depression/basics/symptoms/CON-20032977. Retrieval date: August 7, 2016.

If you are experiencing any of the aforementioned symptoms, take notice and be consistent with your self-care. Take time for yourself to recharge your batteries. You may even need to seek out a counselor for yourself. You are no help to anyone if you are living an emotionally drained life.

6 You are not enough — know that you are not enough. The love, help, support, and care you provide for your loved one is important, but the support for your loved one should not rest entirely on your shoulders. You need to maintain healthy boundaries for yourself and bring in more people who can offer help in unique ways that you may not have thought of or are aware of. It has been said, "It takes a village to raise a child." Well, it also takes a village to help a depressed person recover. Help your loved on seek out support structures for themselves so that you aren't the only lifeline. Support structures can be anything: a faith community, pastoral care, support groups, clubs, online gamer affiliations, depression forums, friends, family members, treatment groups, or mental health professionals.

7 Work with mental health professionals. Mental health professionals are trained in evidence-based treatments that can help those suffering from mental health disorders like depression. Counselors have expertise in depression and are effective in treating the disorder. In addition to counseling, taking medication prescribed and monitored by a psychiatrist

is effective. Counselors also often run group therapy for clients with depression. These treatments
work best in combination.

8 Be informed. Learning as much as you can
about the nature of depression can only
help you and your loved one. Read, study,
and research the causes of depression,
the biology of depression, symptoms, and
treatments. Some of the most identified causes are:[22]

- Stressful events such as the death of a loved
  one, unemployment, childhood trauma, divorce, or domestic abuse

- A chronic medical condition such as diabe-
  tes, heart disease, or cancer

- Parents, siblings, or other family members
  with a history of depression

- Drug or alcohol abuse

Understanding the cause can help you as a family member or significant other to support your
loved one. They may have depression that is root-
ed in a medical condition. If that's the case, they
need to see a doctor. If they are depressed due to
a drug addiction, they may need to be checked in
at an inpatient drug and alcohol treatment facility
or see a chemical dependency counselor for services
at an outpatient facility. If the cause is stress, they
may need to see a counselor to work on effective
stress-management strategies. Identifying the cause
of depression can be helpful in its treatment.

---

[22] https://www.drugs.com/cg/depression.html.   Retrieval   date:
September 5, 2016.

9 Adjust your expectations. Recognize that your loved one may not have the same goals, ambitions, drive, or passion as they once had before depression. You will need to adjust your expectations. You won't be able to depend on them in the same way you once did. The support, love, and affection you received from them won't be as readily available as it once was due to their symptoms or even efforts to overcome the illness. Depression makes people forgetful, absent minded, and lethargic. If you send them out shopping, they may come back without some of the items you requested. In social settings, they may not be as entertaining as they once were. This is not their fault. Don't hold it against them merely adjust your expectations.

10 Maintain hope. The worst thing you can do is lose hope. Your loved one needs you now more than ever. They may be hopeless, but they can lean on your hope and belief and recovery from depression is possible, people do it every day. It takes a lot of hard work, patience, trial and error, treatment, and community support — but it *is* possible. The way towards recovery may seem unclear but trust the process.

Thinking Errors that Negatively Impact Families

Thinking errors are systematic mistakes in one's thinking that apply to every area of life, including how we think about family and our family members. Thinking errors can create a great deal of damage in families because they are not rational. A person who has irrational expectations, perceptions, and responses towards and about their family members can create significant distress within their relationships. Here are **15** common thinking errors:

Filtering: Cognitive Distortions, or thinking errors, are flawed ways of thinking not obvious to an individual, but contribute to unhealthy behaviors. In this list, I share **15** distortions beginning with *Filtering*, which is selectively paying attention to one thing over another, like only focusing on the negative versus the positive.

All or Nothing: A person or event is either *this* or *that*. It is either *good* or *bad*. There is no in-between. This kind of thinking is rigid and inflexible. It is a preference for simplicity over nuance, which may lead a person into believing inaccurate and unjustified conclusions.

Overgeneralization: A person takes one experience and concludes all other experiences will be like the first. For example, if you have an unpleasant experience with a waitress at a restaurant, you conclude that all waitresses are difficult. That is an irrational and logically unjustifiable conclusion because you are taking a limited set of data and making an extrapolation. It could be that most waitresses are pleasant, and you just happened to encounter a bad apple.

Jumping to Conclusions: "Jumping to Conclusions" is like the "Overgeneralization" thinking error in that a person makes an unjustified conclusion. Where the cognitive distortions differ is that "Overgeneralization" is taking one experience or piece of information that is true, but then applying it to all future experiences and information, which is irrational. Whereas in "Jumping to Conclusions," there is no experience or information. Someone is simply arriving at a conclusion based on no information.

Castrophizing: A person gives a negative event greater significance than it deserves. Another way of putting it is "Making a mountain out of a mole hill." For example, if someone is driving in slow, irritating traffic on their way to work, they falsely believe it's an indication of how the rest of their day will go — one bad thing will lead to another, resulting in everything being ruined.

Personalizing: A person who interprets feedback, social interactions and interpersonal experiences in such a way that everything is about them. For example, if a mom gives feedback to her son about his performance when doing a chore, then the son believes his mom is critiquing him. Or when an employee receives their annual performance evaluation and believes their boss doesn't like them because he gave critical feedback about their work. In other words, taking things personally that were not intended to be personal.

Control Fallacy: A person who assumes something is *within* their control when it is not. Foreign affairs, the weather, the stock market (unless you're Bernie Madoff), other people's thoughts, feelings and behaviors are outside your control and you will drive yourself crazy if you try to exert control over them. You'll become an angry *control-freak*. The flipside of this is when someone assumes something is *outside* their control when it isn't. This is the *helpless* person who has the means to change their situation but doesn't because they don't recognize where they have control.

Fallacy of Fairness: A person who believes that at all times they should be treated fairly and with respect. Unfortunately, this is not reality-based thinking. At many times and in many situations, a person will not be treated fairly and with the dignity and respect that is due them.

Blaming: A person who points the finger at everyone else, but takes no responsibility for their own issues or problems. In a family context, for example, this is the person who blames, but doesn't recognize or take ownership for their own contribution to a problem.

Shoulds: A person who has hidden and baseless absolute expectations for how others are to behave. These expectations are not obvious to others and typically don't have a moral or rational basis.

Emotional Reasoning: A person whose feelings override facts. They assume feelings are automatically true. A person assumes the way they are feeling reflects who they must be. For example, if someone interviews for a job and is turned down, they feel like a "loser," which they then interpret as a true and defining statement of themselves.

Fallacy of Change: A person who needs others to change in order to meet their expectations. Their personal wellbeing and happiness is dependent on the other person being a certain way.

Global Labeling: A person who takes an isolated incident, then puts a label on the incident. For example, if your child is dishonest with you, instead of seeing that as a one-time event, you see it as an indication of their character. Your child lied because they must be a liar. This thinking error can lead people into making character assassinations because judgements are made about someone's character based on one or two events.

Always Being Right: A person who assumes that they must always be right. To maintain this assumption, you must rule out the possibility that you could be wrong, that others could know more than you or contradicting information is dismissed. This likely embattles the person in needless fights that are more about their ego than about the facts.

Sunken Cost Fallacy: A person who assumes that investment of time, money, effort or emotions in a relationship, job or project obligates them to continue, even if things are not working.

Here are four steps to overcome thinking errors.

1 Identify the thinking error. Thinking errors can relate to anything. Whatever the error is, you can't change it until you become aware of it. And you need to become aware of it when it's affecting you in the moment, in real time.

Example: *black-and-white thinking*. This thinking error sees people, events, and experiences in rigid, binary categories: everyone and everything is either *this* or *that*, good or bad, honest or dishonest, fun or boring. In the family context, for instance, a parent might see their child as a "bad" kid because they broke trust.

2 Understand how the thinking error makes you feel and behave. Distorted thinking drives distorted feelings and behaviors. Therefore, you need to understand how the distorted thinking influences you.

Example: Because they think of their child as categorically "bad," the parent dismisses everything the child does that doesn't fit within that category meaning that they aren't able to acknowledge any "good" behaviors On the other hand, whatever the child does that fits the category garners exaggerated attention from the parent. This builds resentment in the child towards his parent and they drift further and further apart.

3 Find reasons and evidence that support or counter the thinking error. When you've identified what the thinking error is and how it affects you, the next step is to challenge the thinking error. That means you need to rationally work through both reasons that support the thinking error and considerations that counter it.

Example: challenge the assumption that your child is categorically "bad." First, find supporting evidence: broken trust, poor choices. Second, find counterevidence such as attempts to restore trust, good decisions, healthy behaviors.

4 Conclude with reality-based, accurate, positive thinking. Weigh the supporting evidence against the counterevidence and let that determine your thinking.

Example: *No one is categorically bad. My child has made some good and some bad choices. I need to affirm him for what he does that is good as well as correct him for the bad. This evidence doesn't support a rigid, good or bad, kind of thinking. I can no longer put my child in an oversimplified category of "bad."*

5 Choose new behaviors in line with the new thinking. Distorted thinking ruins opportunities, keeps you from new experiences, and steals your joy. Accurate, reality-based thinking liberates you to enjoy life and to be mentally healthy. Healthy thinking leads to healthy feeling and behaving. Challenging thinking errors leads to an accurate perception of the world — of others and yourself.

Example: *I commit to affirming my son when he does something positive. I will be balanced in what I pay attention to and respond to.*

If you are interested in learning more information about thinking errors and how they relate to family functioning, and more specifically how they affect parents, please check out my book *When Parenting Backfires*, co-authored with David Simonsen, PhD. You can find out more in the "More From Daniel Bates" section at the end of this book.

7 Ways to Make Your Blended Family a Success

Creating unity in a blended family can be difficult. There is emotional baggage, old habits, alliances, norms, and expectations created by the previous family dynamics that could undermine the unity of the new family. Everyone will have to be flexible and open to change since a new normal is being created. Here are 7 guidelines to make your blended family a success.

1 **Define Expectations:** Creating a sense of belonging with your new family is something that each member wants and needs. But how do you create that sense of belonging? When each person in the family is given the opportunity to express their expectations of everyone else, and those expectations are valued, the result is a sense of ownership and belonging. The more someone feels invested in the family, the more they feel that sense of belonging. If individuals don't feel that sense of belonging, it's because their concerns and expectations haven't been taken seriously.

2 **Negotiate Expectations:** When everyone has had a chance to share their expectations, there may be some disagreement if an expectation is to be honored or not. Sometimes someone's expectation may conflict with another person's, but remind yourself that this is not a crisis, but an opportunity for everyone to practice good listening and respectful negotiation. If the kids want a later bedtime during the weekends, instead of having a ready answer, let them make a case for that expectation. Then, both parties should be open to counter-offers and compromises. There may be some expectations that are a hard "yes" or "no," but you may be surprised by how many expectations are negotiable. When negotiation is done well, family members feel a greater sense of belonging, investment and connection to the new family unit.

3 **Feet in Both Camps:** A strong connection to one family is not a rejection of another. What does that mean, practically speaking? An individual may feel a stronger connection to one family versus the other. And that's okay and rather normal in blended families. That should not be seen as a threat to the new family being created. You are not betraying one family by engaging, participating, or enjoying the new family and vice versa. Grant your children the opportunity to explore this topic and be open to talking about this very subject. Your children need to know and you shouldn't necessarily wait for them to bring it up.

4 **Grace:** Give each other grace. There are going to mishaps, stepping on each other's toes, and mistakes. Forming a new family unit is not an easy process. Grace allows relationships to be elastic when stretched and when you blend two families there will be stretching. The grace that will help your family make blending possible, will also enable your family to go the distance. So, take the opportunity to make grace the foundation and culture of your new family.

5 **Comparisons:** Comparing one family to another can be dangerous. I encourage families to find and focus on the merits of *each* family they are a member of and not use the strengths of one as ammunition against the other. It's far too easy to make comparisons and complain. Take the high road and find value where you can.

6 **Cooperation:** Divorce and separation don't truly cut one person off from another, especially when there are kids involved. You will still need to cooperate with the person you are divorced or separated from. If you want to minimize the potential for toxicity, you will have to get along with that person for the benefit of the kids involved. That means communicating well, co-parenting effectively, and limiting your expression of negativity regarding the other person. When these practices are not in place, kids are the ones who suffer the most and often the relationships with both parents will suffer.

7 **Middleman:** Do not, I repeat, do not make your kids the middleman between you and your former spouse or partner. There is nothing more damaging for a child then having to be the mediator between their divorced or separated parents. Let me be clear – *Be an* adult. Being the adult and co-parenting effectively to create the best possible situation for your kids and models for them how to succeed in having healthy relationships.

There are no two ways about it, blending families together is hard working, but the rewards are definitely worth pursuing. Having a clear understanding of expectations, being open to negotiation, allowing family members to give allegiance to both families, eliminating negative comparisons, getting along, giving grace, and avoiding making the children the mediators will help the cohesion of your blended family blossom successfully.

.

About the Author

Daniel Bates is a licensed mental health counselor who works with families dealing with violence, substance abuse, and legal issues. He's passionate about writing and reading poetry, discussing philosophy/theology, spending time with his wife and daughters, connecting with friends, and getting lost in a good book. He's fascinated by the intersection of faith/spirituality and mental health. He's written several books ranging in topic from parenting, families, Christian spirituality and comic book hero psychology, all of which are available on Amazon in Kindle, paperback, and Audible. Daniel also writes for two online magazines: mum.info and FamilyShare.com, in addition to his own blog. You can find links to Daniel's books, read his blog, and view and purchase his paintings at his website, counselordan.com.

More from Daniel Bates

The Modern Mystic

Wish your spiritual life wasn't mediocre? Is your prayer life dead? Are you jealous of the spiritual vitality that everyone else seems to have except for you? Don't let your life be ruled by a spiritual malaise. Instead of checking out, go further and deeper into the heart of God.

But how?

The Christian mystics are ancient voices with a modern message. They teach that the love of God is deeper, wider, and further beyond anything you can understand. It is altogether mysterious and right in front of you. It is the paradoxical truth wrapped in the unimaginable love of a relational God eager to know and be known by you.

Yes, you are the object of God's love. And yes, God is the ultimate source of your happiness. Knowing and experiencing God's love will change you. Yet experiencing God's love is not a destination. It is a journey. And you are a sojourner in need of a guide. Allow the Christian mystics to direct you along the sometimes confusing, wandering path of God's love.

When Parenting Backfires

Let's be honest. Parenting is hard. From the moment children take their first breaths, parents are faced with decisions and choices that no manual could ever fully explain. And the way you parent is constantly changing: babies need protection, toddlers need direction, and teens need influence. We as parents are simply expected to do it and do it well.

From two therapists who have a combined 25 years of experience working with families comes a new kind of parenting book. This book doesn't focus on technique, a discipline scheme, or parenting style. This book focuses on the parent themselves, specifically the kind of thinking that makes parents effective or ineffective. *When Parenting Backfires* examines 12 thinking errors commonly made by parents. In each chapter, Dan and David:

- Explain the thinking error

- Analyze how it backfires

- Examine what parents can do to correct the thinking error

- Offer real-life examples of parents who have recognized their thinking error, made the correction, and improved their effectiveness

Let this book do its work. Let down your guard and be open to the new ideas. The biggest risk you'll take is to your ego as you improve your parenting skills and your relationship with your kids. I think any effective parent is willing to take those odds. Are you?

Learning to Live

You are the reason you are stuck.

You can either stay stuck or learn how to get un-stuck. In order to get un-stuck, you must engage in the learning process. That means learning about your-self, your perceptions, your thinking, your communica-tion style, and how you view relationships. But learning is hard to do without some help. Fortunately, an experienced therapist, Daniel Bates, has compiled **20** lessons based on his clinical experience and the latest social science research to help you.

Learning to Live will help you engage with the lifelong work of learning. Learning isn't an event; it's a journey. It can be painful, challenging at times, and downright uncomfortable, but the end result is worth it. Lessons have a way of sticking with you for the rest of your life. They are the gift that keeps on giving. So what are you waiting for? Start learning so you can start living.

Even a Superhero Needs Counseling

Even a Superhero Needs Counseling is an in-depth guide to understanding your favorite comic book character from a psychological perspective that also provides you with relevant and insightful advice. In other words, by learning more about Thor, the Hulk, Wonder Woman, Stephen Strange, Superman, and  many more, you can learn more about yourself. Comic books aren't just entertainment; they can be a window into the strengths and weaknesses of humanity.

Daniel Bates is a licensed mental health counselor who offers his expert counsel for superhero, super-villain, and reader alike. In each chapter, you'll find:

- An overview of a major comic book character's origin story, arch-enemies, and psychological dynamics

- A mental health diagnosis based on the relevant details of the character's symptoms

- What mental health treatment would consist of based on the diagnosis and how it would help their life

- And most importantly, how your favorite comic book character's story can be informative for your own personal growth

So if you struggle with anxiety, you're in good company — Superman can relate. If you've had an addiction, you and Tony Stark could go to an Alcoholics Anonymous meeting together. Or if you've ever had relationship problems, the Scarlet Witch can commiserate with you. Whatever the problem, you will find a superhero or super-villain that shares your struggle. And through their stories, you can find help for yours.

Podcasts and Blog from Daniel

Counselor Dan Podcast is a podcast for those who want to be entertained and informed. The Podcast goes deep into the latest research from psychology, provides helpful insights from counseling, and gives the personal experiences Daniel has accrued over his career. You can find the podcast at counselor-danpodcast.com.

Daniel also co-hosts a podcast with author and therapist David Simonsen, PhD. The podcast focuses on mental health, relational and emotional growth, and pop culture. Dan and David take calls from listeners with relational and mental health questions, interview special guests, review movies, and analyze the political landscape through the lens of a therapist.

Check Out Daniel's Website

Daniel's blog, videos, books, and information about counseling services can be found on his website, counselordan.com. The website is a fantastic resource for anyone interested in psychology and mental health. New blogs, podcasts and videos are added to the site every week. You can discover information on how to book Daniel for speaking engagements, counseling services and interviews.

Counseling Services

If you are interested in contacting Daniel for counseling, he recently expanded his private practice at Lacamas Counseling in Camas, Washington. You can find information about Daniel's counseling specialties, as well as the location of the office or of other counselors that may be a fit for you at lacamascounseling.com. He's currently accepting new clients. Email or call to schedule an appointment.